The Power of Miracle Metaphysics

Also by the Author:

How to Reduce and Control Your Weight Through Self Hypnotism, Sidney Petrie and Robert B. Stone, Prentice-Hall, Inc. (1965).

Martinis and Whipped Cream: The New Carbo-Cal Way to Lose Weight and Stay Slim, Sidney Petrie and Robert B. Stone, Parker Publishing Company, Inc. (1966).

How to Strengthen Your Life with Mental Isometrics, Sidney Petrie and Robert B. Stone, Parker Publishing Company, Inc. (1968).

Lazy Lady's Easy Diet—A Fast-Action Plan to Lose Weight Quickly for Sustained Slenderness and Youthful Attractiveness, Sidney Petrie and Robert B. Stone, Parker Publishing Company, Inc. (1969).

Conduct Your Own Awareness Sessions, Christopher Hills and Robert B. Stone, New American Library (1970).

Miracle Diet for Fast Weight Loss, Sidney Petrie and Robert B. Stone, Parker Publishing Company, Inc. (1970).

What Modern Hypnotism Can Do For You, Sidney Petrie and Robert B. Stone, Hawthorn (1968), Fawcett (1972).

Hypno-Cybernetics: Helping Yourself to a Rich New Life, Sidney Petrie and Robert B. Stone, Parker Publishing Company, Inc. (1973).

Jesus Has A Man In Waikiki, Revell (1973).

Fat Destroyer Foods: The Magic Metabolizer Diet, Sidney Petrie and Robert B. Stone, Parker Publishing Company, Inc. (1974).

For Once In My Life, Connie Haines and Robert B. Stone, Warner (1976).

The Power of Miracle Metaphysics

Robert B. Stone

Parker Publishing Company, Inc.

West Nyack, NewYork

Library of Congress Cataloging in Publication Data

Stone, Robert B.
    The power of miracle metaphysics.

    1. Occult sciences.   2. Success.   I. Title.
BF1411.S85   133   75-28309
ISBN 0-13-686683-2

Printed in the United States of America

Dedication

This book is dedicated to the
Universal Consciousness
which expresses itself through all beings and things
and which the reader learns to use herein to enhance
and accelerate personal and universal progress.

What This Book Will Do for You

This book introduces you to the miraculous metaphysical powers within you *right now*, by giving you the methods you need to put them into positive action.

In a few days you can be demonstrating these powers in many ways. If I tell you in what ways now it will astound you. But these incredible happenings will become commonplace for you by the time you finish this book.

You will find that you can:

- Get as much money as you want.
- Read other people's thoughts.
- See through walls even miles away.
- Influence people to do your bidding.
- Reap a crop of good luck every day.
- Revitalize your health and postpone aging.
- Protect yourself from those who are "out to get you."
- Climb the social, political, or business ladder to undreamed success.
- Affect world events.
- Buy or sell the right stocks at the right time.

Some have been able to use these techniques to transcend scientific law, as we understand science today, to change the weather, transport objects instantly over vast distances, convert cheap metal to precious metal, and be in two places at once, among other miraculous events.

You may not want to go that far. But the methods are all here if you do.

You can learn to use your metaphysical power in a few minutes. Long before you finish this book, you will be able to prove to yourself that you are indeed able to do the impossible time after time.

A man acquires a million dollar fortune. A woman wins the perfect soul-mate. He finds a job. She wins a lottery. Illnesses disappear. Fantastic "coincidences" occur as if on a timetable.

Would you like to have everything your heart desires, as I do? Have all the money you need to do anything you'd like to do, as I have? Feel wonderful and look twenty years younger than your age, as I do? Have men and women idolize you, work short hours, play at what you enjoy most—all your "good fortune"?

I am ready now to share with you the metaphysical secrets I have tested successfully in my life and which have been tested successfully by others.

If you and others learn to apply your metaphysical powers, this can be a better world.

I want you to be able to have anything you want—a new house, a car, a television set, an electronic computer, a yacht. I want you to be able to have things go your way—with your mate, with your family, with your business or your boss, with your neighbors, with your friends. I want you to be healthy, happy, vital, creative, and important.

And there's no reason why I can't, once again, manifest what I want—in you.

There's no hocus-pocus to this. It's a no-nonsense program to extend your present conscious ability manyfold—something like extending the antenna of your radio for more efficient results.

My studies at the Massachusettes Institute of Technology have enabled me to understand and harness metaphysical energy in ways that we, in the West can relate to. No mystical rites. No weird ceremonies. Just simple but very special, uses of human consciousness.

It all starts with an easy-to-learn process known as *alpha picturing*—you learn it by sitting quietly in a chair and daydreaming in a special manner. It goes on to other just as easy applications of your conscious energy—the superphysical, wonder-working energy that you have always had but never could quite control.

This energy is recognized now by scientists all over the world. They are studying it, using it. The science is called psychotronics.

By controlling this energy you can create miracle after miracle in your life. Little miracles like the woman who found a lost will, the man who manifested a car for his use, the executive who stopped his competitors dead in their tracks. Or, major miracles like creating a continuing flow of riches, locating a lost treasure, or checking secret documents miles away without leaving your living room.

- "I got the urge to play the number six and I won!"
- "I stopped getting headaches and dizzy spells. I feel better than I ever remember feeling."
- "It came in the mail. It was exactly the information I needed. I don't know who sent it."
- "He asked me out to dinner. Me, of all people. It was a magical evening."
- "I've tripled my profits this year."
- "We're leaving on a trip around the world."
- "He's retiring and asking the board to name me as his successor."

These people talking are people who have practiced using their mind in a special metaphysical way. It can be you talking. Here is exactly what this book shows you:

1. It helps you to go quickly and easily to a level of mind where the mind produces exactly what it wants.
2. It enables you to keep your miracle-making batting average high.
3. It shows you how to use this ability to help yourself to better health, all the money you'll ever need, a totally great new life.
4. It gives you the means to use this ability to help others or to control others for mutual good, to bring them what you want them to have.
5. It directs you how to use this ability to change life's circumstances around you, to make everything happen for the best.

You are able to use your consciousness as if it were the prime mover of the universe. You discover that where your consciousness goes, energy goes—a powerful energy that, although as yet unmeasured as electricity went unmeasured and uncontrolled for centuries, can:

- Bring back information to you about events that have not happened yet.

- Enable you to see what a person is doing thousands of miles away.
- Penetrate skin and flesh to detect malfunctioning in a body and then cause spiritual healing.
- Build an impenetrable wall around you to protect you from others with malicious design.
- Invest stones or gems with the power to be good luck talismans.
- Imbue commands with a power impossible to oppose.
- Cause life energy to flow through your body for astounding endurance.
- Work a pendulum to locate best markets or mineral veins.
- Give you judgment to make the right decision time after time.
- Increase your metaphysical powers day after day.

Now this energy can be harnessed by you. You have had it all along but you have been using it correctly only occasionally. Once this energy is harnessed, life becomes quite a different road. Everything goes the way you want it to. What you can "see" happening, happens.

Now this road is open to you. You can begin the cavalcade of miracles by just *turning the page.*

You use simple conscious energy. Whatever you desire comes to you. The reams of cash. The ecstacy of love. The power to control, dominate, succeed.

Can you "see" it happening?

Then, you're very close to making it happen.

Turn.

Robert B. Stone

ACKNOWLEDGMENTS

My eternal gratitude to the metaphysicians, philosophers, gurus, and Masters who, by their presence or written word, have imparted to me what now belongs to all who are ready for it.

A special word of thanks goes to Dr. Jacques Bustanoby, wherever he is, for having been the first to show me who I am; to Christopher Hills of Boulder Creek, California, for his spiritual insights; and to Dr. Jose Silva of Laredo, Texas, for his research and teaching in the realm of the subjective mind.

Contents

xiii

How to Get Lady Luck to Work Full Time for You

The Three Levels of Good Fortune That You Can Now Claim

How to Get Out of Your Own Way and Permit Good Luck to Flow

Make Room in Your Life for Great Happenings

How to Put Your Hat in the Ring for the Really Big Rewards

The Miraculous Link Between You and the Universe

Metaphysical Action Plan

For Getting Out of Your Own Way

For Making Space in Your Life for Good Luck

For Good Luck Reinforcement

For Harnessing Cosmic Power in Your Life

Case Examples

The Man Who Got Rid of Shyness

How to Put Charms and Incantations to Work for You

The Seal of Solomon Magnifies Your Power of Attraction

The Role the Swastika Can Play in Your Love Life

How to Whisper Magic Words That Act as Love Commands

The Secret That Can Make the Opposite Sex Swarm Around You Like a Hungry Mob

Turn Up Your Sexual Attraction with Those Powerful Commands

How to Use the Hypnotic Eye on Members of the Opposite Sex

Metaphysical Action Plan

For Attracting Back a Loved One

For Attracting a Person to Your Side with Solomon's Seal

To Add Life to Your Romance with the Swastika

For Using Words That Act as Love Commands

Case Examples

How Stephen R. Used a Piece of Her Clothing to Attract Her to Him

How Roland L. Used Whispered Commands to Trigger Her Passionate Response

For Acquiring Intensified Sexual Attraction

To Use the Hypnotic Eye

How Betty L. Changed Her Boy
Friend's Hostility into Endear-
ment in Hours

A Powerful Mantra that Materialized Money

The Wheel of Fortune and How to Make It Spin a Fortune for You

How to Energize a Dollar Bill to Multiply Manyfold Again and
Again

How to Multiply the Deluge of Money by Combining Your Power
with Others

How to Keep Money Flowing to You from Many Directions

Can You Discover the Ancient Secret of Turning Base Metals into
Gold?

Give the Universe Carte Blanche to Bestow Wealth on You

Metaphysical Action Plan

To Change from a Consciousness of Poverty to One of
Wealth

For Energizing a Wheel of
Fortune

To Charge Up a Dollar Bill to
Set Off an Explosion of Money

To Build Up Conscious Energy
by Joining with Others

Case Examples

How Pamela B. Used a One
Dollar Bill to Start a Flow of
Thousands

How Steve B. Used Affirmation
and Mantra for a Life of Ease

How Mrs. Norman E. Made a
$3,000 Commission with a
Charged $1 Bill

How Mrs. Evelyn V.'s Image
of a Home Backfired

How Sam J. Won a $50,000
Lottery

How to Correct Errors in Your Internal Health Make

Enter the Cells of Your Body and Imbue Them with Youth and
Radiance

How to Rid Yourself of the Aging Habit While Your Friends Move
On in Years

Seven Tips for Metaphysical Protection

Metaphysical Action Plan	*Case Examples*
For Creating a Protective Shield of L I G H T	How Mrs. Patricia A. Protected Herself from Gangsters
To Pick Up Voices from Another Plane	How Gregory B. Enlisted Higher Energies to Come to His Aid
To Enlist Protection from Another Plane	How Mrs. Mary C. Threw Off a Five Year Psychic Attack
For Strengthening the Shadow Body to Prevent Energy-Sucking	How Sam T. Changed His Life Once He Discovered He Was His Own Psychic Attacker
To Identify Drug Takers Through Radiesthesia	How I Blocked the Probing of Another Metaphysician

How to Penetrate the Cosmic Mind Where All Knowledge Lies

Miracles You Can Now Perform with a Simple Pendulum

How to Determine if There Is Any Money Hidden in Your House or Buried Nearby

How to Probe Cosmic Consciousness for Best Business Locations and Marketing Opportunities

Find Veins of Gold, Mineral Deposits, and Buried Treasure

Miraculous Answers That the Pendulum Can Provide

Metaphysical Action Plan	*Case Examples*
To Marry Your Consciousness with Cosmic Consciousness	How Miss Naomi U. Found Lost Documents
To Put the Pendulum to Work for You	How Shipwrecked People Were Located with a Pendulum After Planes Had Given Up the Search
To Locate Hidden Money or Valuables	
To Determine Best Street Location for a Retail Store	How Captain Alex J. Used the Pendulum to Find Evidence of the Lost Continent Atlantis
To Locate Gold, Silver, and	

How to Use the Secret of the Five Pointed Star to Magnify Your
Metaphysical Powers

How to Induce Signals from Another Dimension

How to Rev Up Your Desire for the High Voltage Power You Need
to Attain It

The Intellect of a Genius Is Only a Few Brain Waves Away for You

How to Add a New Dimension to Alpha Picturing to Escalate Its
Power

How to Create Magic Talismans with Strange Powers

Metaphysical Action Plan

To Become a Star Among Men

To Concentrate Universal
Energy At a Point in Your Body

To Add Irresistible Voltage to
Your Desire

To Automatically Deepen Alpha
Levels

To Use the Power of Your
Consciousness to Create a
Talisman

Case Examples

How Karl J. Saw Proof of ESP
but Denied It

One Place Where the Secret Star
Action Works Every Day

How John G. Heated Up His
Desires and Found Work Immediately

How Dr. Jacques B. Found a
Rare Book by Using His Breath

How I "Talked" to Helen and

Metaphysical Action Plan	*Case Examples*
To Sensitive Intuitive Reception	How Nicholas Tesla Listened to the Universe's Secrets and Patented Them
To Bring Auras More Clearly into View	
To Use a Television Set, Clock, and Calendar to See the Future	How Sterling B. Saw an Aura That Saved the Day for Him
To Surpass the Greatest Person That You Know of in Your Field	Stephen B. Saw the Outcome of the Trial a Year Ahead
To Survive a Cataclysm or Accident	How Michele B. Survived What Could Have Been a Fatal Crash
	How Harry Houdini Called on Superhuman Forces to Save Him

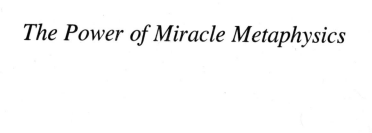

The Power of Miracle Metaphysics

1

The Strongest Power in Your Life and How It Can Work Miracles for You Consistently

Man has discovered a new form of energy. Just as atomic energy towers over electricity, so does this new energy tower over atomic energy. The amazing thing about this new energy is that you do not need to build any costly atom reactors or electrical generators to use it.

We already have that energy source. And it is free. Man has discovered that *consciousness is energy*. Throughout the world scientists are tooling up to study conscious energy in the laboratory. They have already found that human consciousness can create and destroy matter. They have found that human consciousness can go any place on this planet and retrieve information. They have already found that one person's consciousness can affect another person's consciousness.

You have consciousness. You are conscious of this book in your hand, of the meaning of the words you are reading. The promise of mystics, practitioners of the occult, and ancient seers that miracles can happen is now a step closer to scientific understanding. Yes, you can make miracles happen in your life—a torrent of money, a surge of popularity, a wave of good fortune, "impossible" feats—day after day.

You have had your consciousness right along. Why have you been unable to cause these miracles up until now? The answer is that conscious energy needs to be harnessed and directed in a special way. Electricity was around long before Ben Franklin, but it never so much as lighted a bulb. In this book I tell you how to use your consciousness so that its energy produces what you want.

Mr. E.W. learned to use his consciousness in this special way. He wanted, among other things, to be a millionaire. Using this system, he got an idea for a new enterprise, quit his work as a management consultant, organized the new firm, and inside of two years had not only netted a million dollars but was headed for continuing millions.

Miss L.M. used her consciousness in a special way to attract a mate. She ran a dress shop in California, dated frequently, but held out for the mature, intelligent man she knew would be right for her. Within one year, she met a district court judge and they were married.

I was in the process of teaching a South American mother of five to tap her conscious energy. A divorcee, she wanted to return to her country. She had taken only two brief lessons when she was faced with a cashless weekend. She sat comfortable in a chair, and used her mind in a special way. Within one minute, one of her children ran into the house exclaiming, "Look, Mama, I found it blowing across the lawn."

"It" was a ten dollar bill.

Fast and easy made electricity popular.

Fast and easy stands to make your natural energy of consciousness even more popular.

The Easiest Thing You
Ever Learned to Do in Your Life

In school you learned many things, some difficult, some easy. You used your mind. But that's one thing they never *taught* in school—how to use your mind. Using your mind is so easy. It comes naturally.

Well, using your mind in this special way is also easy. There is actually nothing to it. Opening a locked safe is easy too—if you have the combination. If you do not have the combination, you can try hour after hour, day after day, week after week, and get nowhere.

Indeed, most people go through a lifetime and never hit on the mental "combination." They brush by it occasionally and a good thing happens in their life. Then the bad weather returns and they wonder why.

Most safes have a number of dials to turn. Opening them can be a six, eight, or ten step process. "Four turns to the right to number 35, three turns to the left to number 28." The system is designed to make the odds insurmountable that you might happen on the correct procedure by chance.

The secret for tapping the energy of consciousness protects riches greater than any safe could store. Yet it is such a simple procedure that even a child can learn it. In fact, children come upon it frequently. They "see" things that we cannot see. They know things they could not possibly know. Then we talk them out of it with "It's just your imagination," or we grill them in third degree fashion with "Now who told you that—where did you hear that?"

I predict that many "impossible" things that you learn to do in the chapters ahead will sound strangely familiar to you. Like you are being reminded of what you once knew.

You did know. But your family and teachers ridiculed, taunted, threatened, and cajoled. It became easier to see things their way. Goodbye ESP.

Centuries ago, some of this knowledge about conscious energy was in the hands of philosophers and physicians. It was so powerful though that they kept it secret. They figured that the average person was not ready to use it. One of these forebearers of metaphysics was Hermes. His secrets were so closely guarded that the word "hermetic" has come to mean tightly sealed.

We must be ready for them now because the occult is being de-occulted. No more secrets. Metaphysics is becoming just plain physics. The responsibility to use this new energy creatively not destructively is still yours. Just like you better know how to handle that light socket before you shove anything into it.

It is amazing how simple the secrets are to learn. All you need to do is read the first three chapters of this book. It is all here. The rest of the book just tells you how to use what you learned.

When you learned multiplication tables you had to work harder than you will have to work now. This is as easy as sitting in a chair and relaxing. In fact, that is one of the steps. And do you know how many steps there are? Just one more.

Don't get me wrong. There is more to it. Once you memorized multiplication tables, you had to find out what they were for. Soon you learned how to use what seemed useless. You could know how many pennies you would need to buy six five-cent lollipops.

The two easy-as-pie steps are covered in the first three chapters. But I need 13 more chapters to tell you how to use your new energy of consciousness to:

- Check out another person and find out where they are, whom they are with, and what they are doing.
- Create a "wall" of protection for yourself from would-be attackers.
- Invest a stone or amulet with special power that works for you wherever you go.
- Start abundance flowing into your life in the form of possessions, luxuries, and cash.
- Improve your health, youthfulness, and sexuality so that you behave like a new person.
- Change your life in scores of other ways.

How This New Energy
Works Metaphysical Miracles

Electricity could never have been used for power if man had not created machines and appliances that permitted electrical energy to do its work—the electric grill, radio, washing machine, and television being some common examples.

The power of consciousness, easy to generate, also needs outlets, but of a different sort, in order to do its work. Do you remember stories of how he used a lock of her hair to win her back to him? Or how she had a piece of clothing of his that she used to attract him back to her? Or how Haitian voodoo uses pins and a doll or likeness to do its dirty work?

You will have no need to do dirty work. It will be too easy to make everything happen for the best—you will not even think about doing harm to anybody.

But you will learn to provide some simple aids for the energy of consciousness to work through—like the power-packed stone or amulet mentioned a moment ago, or the pendulum that pierces time and space to tell you what to expect in the future, or where to find oil, water, or valuable underground resources.

You are the generator of your energy of consciousness. This energy then works through you, your friends, and objects you designate.

Czechoslovakian scientists have been reported to be able to store this energy of consciousness. A person can stare into a specially shaped container which collects and stores his "stare" energy. That energy can then be made to turn a wheel. But that's not all.

The person can sit in one room with the container and wheel in the next room. If four different types of fruit are placed in front of him and if those same types of fruit are placed around the container with a pointer attached to the wheel, when the person stares at one type of fruit in one room, the wheel points to that same type of fruit in the next room.

Incredible. But those are the kinds of incredible things that keep happening when you harness your energy of consciousness.

How Power Builds Up in Shapes and Designs Over Long Periods of Time

If people put their conscious energy into a special symbol, that symbol seems to acquire energy to influence lives. Take the five pointed star that you find in the American flag. That symbol has been around for a long time. It has nothing to do with stars you see in the sky. They do not have points. It has to do with man himself—man and his perfection.

Nobody need ever tell anybody this, yet the effect of the star on man will continue to inspire him toward perfection.

There is a very special symbol called Solomon's Seal. It brings two people together. I will tell you how to use it in a later chapter. It has worked for millennia and will continue to do so as long as people who learn to use it keep adding their conscious energy to that symbol.

Then there is La Croix d'Agardes. It is worn by thousands of men and women in France, always next to the skin, to change their destiny for the better and to bring health and happiness. It is purported to have been copied in the eighteenth century in Agardes, a French African territory, where it was worn by the Bedouins for protection and power. It is still spreading in popularity and is now being promoted in the United States.

Too bad that people who acquire talismans do not know how to trigger their real power. A magic charm remains a conversation piece until you use the special method for turning on its metaphysical powers with your own conscious energy.

Then watch the world around you respond to it!

Coincidence? Well, Then, Expect
One Happy Coincidence After Another

A young man phoned me and said, "My girl friend has left me. We have lived together two months and had some disagreements. But I am beside myself. Can you help me find her?" I said I would try.

In five minutes I called him back. I told him the town some ten miles away where she was. "She is not with another man but with relatives or good friends. She misses you. She is already planning on returning. Play it cool."

In five days, his girl friend returned. She was staying with an aunt in that very town.

Coincidence? Lucky guess? Maybe.

But when you use conscious energy, these impossible things become possible. Your friends call it coincidence. And there is no way in the world that you can refute that argument.

So you keep enjoying these "coincidences."

No matter what miracle you can make happen, you can always count on somebody calling it a coincidence. These people are not ready to accept something as dramatically new as these metaphysical changes you can produce. So don't attempt to force them to accept it.

Just continue to perfect your production of this miraculous energy of consciousness and your use of it for creating transformations in your life.

Scientists Know That You
Can Make Matter Appear and Disappear
but They Cannot Even Begin to Explain It

Speaking to a meeting of the Academy of Parapsychology and Medicine in California, Dr. Edward Mitchell, an astronaut who visited the moon and left NASA to create the Institute of Noetic Sciences, told of observing matter made to disappear.

"According to the laws of conservation of energy," he said, "San Francisco and South Bay should have disappeared with it."

According to scientists like Dr. Mitchell, we are on the threshold of conceiving a new cosmology—or scientific picture of the universe—that will accept mind over matter phenomena. Then, instead of scratching their heads and walking away from such happenings or pretending they did not see them, scientists will devise methods for putting these powers of the mind to work to make this a better world to live in.

We go part of the way in this book. We may not make matter disappear and reappear. But we will change its appearance, as in health matters, and increase its flow, as in energy and money matters. "What is mind?" said Socrates. "It is no matter. What is matter? Never mind."

In a California laboratory, scientists are working with people who demonstrate a type of healing power that seems to flow through their hands. A batch of enzyme is prepared. An enzyme is a complex organic substance which induces chemical change in other substances. Its strength or ability to do this, as in digestion, can be measured. The batch is divided in three parts. One is a control and nothing is done to it. A second is damaged by untraviolet light waves. This batch, and the third, are placed between the hands of a healer for a brief time. The damaged second batch and this third batch are measured after the hand treatment and are found to be stronger than the control group.

Is this hand energy the privilege of only special people? Of course not. We are all healers.

Feel Your Own Psychic
Energy in a Physical Way Right Now

I want you to feel something you have never felt before. Give it whatever name you wish. In the Orient, they have called it prana; in Polynesia, they have called it mana. I call it life energy.

It is important that you begin to know more about it. You are going to be working metaphysical "miracles" with it.

Follow these instructions:

Metaphysical
Action Plan
for Feeling
Your
Life Energy

1. Hold your left palm in a vertical position.

2. Place your right palm horizontally with the fingers pointed at the left palm, but with the finger tips at least six inches away, so you do not feel any heat.

3. Now slowly wave the fingers of the right palm up and down as if shooting bullets at the left palm.

4. Immediately you feel a sensation going up and down the left palm.

The sensation you feel is hard to describe. It can be called a tickling feeling, or a tingle, or a warmth. But just about everybody can feel it.

It can now be photographed. A Russian named Kirlian discovered one method, but a number of United States researchers, including Dr. Don Parker, have come up with other methods. The pictures show colored light radiating outward from the fingers. These lights change color as the emotions of the person change. They are called auras.

Some sensitive people can see these auras naturally. Most everybody can train themselves to see them. Begin by looking for a slight discoloration just outside the hair line. We usually discount what we see by thinking it a quirk of vision. Accept what you see and you gradually see the aura better and better around the head.

Then you can tell where somebody's "head is at." Red means highly emotional, orange gregarious, yellow intellectual, green material or health-minded, and blue spiritual.

Whether or not you can see it, feel it, touch it, or smell it, your life energy is very much present. It is not just the energy that runs your body and keeeps you alive. It is the energy of consciousness.

That's where we begin to get into a fuzzy area of knowledge. People confuse the mind and its consciousness with the brain and its thoughts.

The Energy of Consciousness
Towers over Brain Energy

The brain is the gray matter inside our skull. It is visible.

The mind is not material. It is energy. It is invisible.

The brain keeps us alive. The mind directs that aliveness.

The brain is confined to the skull. The mind can go anywhere.

You are not conscious of your brain. It obeys your consciousness but works independently of your consciousness.

For instance, you try to remember the name of that fellow you met a few days ago. Your consciousness seeks to get it from the memory cells of your brain. Your mind cannot reach into those memory cells of your brain and retrieve the name. Hard as you try, no luck. So your mind goes about its business. Then, minutes later, the brain delivers that name to your mind.

The brain has energy. The electrical aspects of this energy are easily measured by an instrument known as the electroencephalograph.

The mind has energy. It cannot be as easily measured. But it can be partially felt as consciousness. Where your consciousness goes, so goes the energy of mind. It is this mind energy, not brain energy, that is the source of metaphysical power—power beyond the ability of physical science to measure.

Your consciousness *is* that power. The consciousness of man has created the civilized world—from the chair you are sitting in, to the book you are holding, to the home you are living in. They all started in the consciousness of man as mental pictures, mental concepts. Then man puts those mental images into words, sketches, designs, working drawings.

Not all mental images get created. But nothing is ever created by man that is not first mentally imaged. Mental imaging comes first. It is man's creative energy.

The brain goes to work next. It learns the skill to use a hammer or saw and provides the energy and muscle coordination to shape and manipulate materials to fit the blueprint. The brain is the tool of the mind.

Now here is where miracles come in. Because your brain can manipulate materials, your consciousness becomes dependent on your brain. It says, "I'll get the ideas, brain, you carry them out. If you cannot carry them out, then I'll just have to give up that idea."

Error. The mind has other ways to get you what you want. If your brain cannot produce a brand new car, permit your mind to use its creative energy through other tools, ways, or channels. For instance . . .

A man decides he needs a car to get started in a sales business. He "sees" that by driving house to house he can build up a clientele for his product. But . . .no money, no credit, no car. He stops "seeing" the car.

Another man in the very same position does not give up. He keeps on "seeing" the car. Then he gets a phone call from a friend. "I'm going away. Can you take care of my car for a month?"

The energy of consciousness seems to be able to reach out to consciousness everywhere. "Coincidences" happen. Before you are very far along in the book, you are going to be able to create happy "coincidence" after happy "coincidence,"—all through the simple process of using your mind pictures in a special way. You may not understand how it works, but then neither did Benjamin Franklin know exactly how electricity worked. Your conscious energy will do for you even more than electricity.

Create an Outpouring of
Extraordinary Events in Your Life

Anything is possible.
I have seen where this mental picturing has been followed by:

● An unexpected business deal worth thousands.

● An invitation to join a firm at nearly double the salary.

● A chance meeting that led to a successful business partnership.

I have seen mental picturing, used in a special way, bring:

● A gift from an unexpected source.

● A change in the weather that permitted the pictured event to occur.

● A dream that contained the answer.

After awhile you are tempted to drop the word "unexpected" from your vocabulary. You expect the pictured result. The only thing that is unexpected is the way that it will arrive.

You create one happy circumstance after another. Gradually, you transform your life. I say "gradually" because it is done image by image.

A seminar is taking place. Some 150 government employees are attending a three day session devoted to more efficient management of their time. The leader asks them to take a minute to write down their lifetime goals. Then he asks them to take another minute to write down what they would like to accomplish in the next five years.

"If you only had six months left to live, what would you want to accomplish in that time?" Again, he gave them about a minute to write. Then he asked them to decide which of their accomplishments would have the most value to them in the next seven days.

You can guess the final question. "Which do you want to start on today?"

This brief activity has great benefit. It is an activity of mental imaging. It images the long range goal, then the first step toward that goal.

It is not daydreaming. It is not mere mental calisthenics. It is imaging. It is like stepping on the starter, then on the accelerator of your car. And away you go.

What did not happen—at least under systematic control—at this seminar, was the imaging of goals in a special way. Then, not only do you travel toward your goal but your goal travels toward you, sometimes at an incredible speed:

- A 45-year-old widow was told by doctors she had a grave disease. She did imaging in a special way. Within eight months she no longer had any sign of the disease and she was happily remarried.

- A free-lance teacher needed more outlets for his courses. He did his special mental picturing. Within two weeks, he had three offers from schools and institutions for his special services.

- A young woman needed an escort to take her to the important social event of the year. She pictured herself there in a special way. Within two days an old friend called and asked to take her.

When You Picture in a Special Way
You Acquire Staggering Abilities That Defy Science

The brain is a marvelous organ made up of billions of cells that communicate with each other and cooperate to form motor and sensory areas. These, in turn, communicate with some thirty billion nerve cells throughout the body including about three million pain signal points along the skin. All input to the body through the nervous system— sight, sounds, emotions, etc.—is recorded in the brain, even from prenatal days.

The mind is an even more marvelous organ. Though made up of no cells, it also communicates. It communicates to the brain and also to other minds. Our mind's consciousness seems to contact the consciousness of the other mind's as if we were all part of the same consciousness.

Much research is now being done along these lines. It started more than a decade ago when parapsychologists conducted a special experiment in New York City. A man and wife, volunteering for the experiment, were placed in separate hospitals some five miles apart. They were each hooked up to devices that measured heart beat, blood pressure, skin galvanic reaction, brain waves and other physiological functioning.

The husband was then approached by one of the parapsychologists who told him somberly that he had bad news. His wife had died suddenly in the experiments. After a ten-second pause, he was then told that his wife was fine, that this was just part of the experiment.

The devices measured the man's shock. Five miles away where the wife was sitting unaware of this, her system also registered a shock.

Somehow the two minds were in communication despite the distance and despite their being unaware of this communication.

Today, we know that man's mind affects plants. Cleve Backster, who worked with the polygraph to demonstrate this again and again to doubting scientists, has now earned his proof of communication of life energy with life energy to this incredible limit: One-celled yogurt bacteria, when fed milk, not only register excitement, but some 50 feet away, another batch of yogurt bacteria echoes that same excitement via automatic encephalograph readings.

The life energy of a single-celled creature communicates across 50 feet. Multiply those 50 feet by the hundreds of billions of cells in your body and you begin to realize that distance does not really matter.

Broadcast your image and the whole world is attuned to it. If you have a need and image it in a special way, it is as if all the ships at sea hear your SOS and the closest one responds with help.

Image your need for money in a special way.

Image your need for health, a house, a car, a baby sitter, a special book, a break, a helping hand, love, a decision in your favor—in a special way.

That image reaches the consciousness that can help. And the image becomes that house, that book, a warm body, or cold cash.

Now—about that special way . . .

2

Alpha Picturing–Key to Harnessing Your Metaphysical Power for Controlled Miracles

Parapsychology is the name given to the science that explores such metaphysical powers of man as clairvoyance, telepathy, precognition and psychokinesis.

The American Association for the Advancement of Science has admitted the Parapsychological Assocation as an affiliate. Also, the National Institute of Mental Health has made a major grant of funds to the Maimonides Hospital in Brooklyn for use by their Division of Parapsychology and Psychophysics.

What you are going to be doing in this chapter is a scientifically accepted technique for developing your metaphysical powers.

No hocus pocus. But a tested methodology for solving your money problems, your office problems, your health problems, your happiness problems.

Take health. A man had several stomach attacks which his doctor said appeared to be gallbladder. X-rays were scheduled. But meanwhile, the man decided to work on himself using the healing power of metaphysics.

Here is what he did. He relaxed. He imagined his gallbladder. Yes, he "saw" gravel in it. He saw the gravel leaving and the gallbladder restored to healthy functioning. Within three days he had a very painful few hours. But when X-rays were taken, they showed a normal gallbladder. The man has not had any such trouble to this day.

KNOW METHOD
IS SOUND
↓
EXPECT POSITIVE
RESULTS
↓
RELAX
↓
USE IMAGING
POWER
↓
EXPECT A
"MIRACLE"

What actually happened? First, the person had to know this method is sound, and to expect positive results. You cannot hide negative expectations from your mind, because that's where they reside. Expect failure and you create failure.

Second, the person had to relax. Now this sounds easy, but most people do not know how to relax except when they go to sleep.

Third, the person used the imaging power of his mind in a certain way.

Period. That's all there was to it. Except to sit back and expect a "miracle."

The Two Step Method for Acquiring Awesome Metaphysical Power

A man sits quietly with his eyes closed. In a moment, the telephone rings.

"Hello."

"Bill, this is Virginia. I just happened to feel like calling you. How are you?"

Of course, Virginia just happened to feel like calling him. He was visualizing her picking up the telephone and dialing his number.

It need not have happened that fast, but happen it must.

A woman sits quietly with her eyes closed. In a few minutes, she gets up and goes for an interview. There is a fine rapport between the interviewer and herself. She lands the job.

Of course, she lands the job. She was visualizing a successful interview and a quick decision in her favor.

Whether Virginia is right for the man or the job is right for the woman is a factor in the result, but more likely not the deciding factor.

You are still responsible for making a proper judgment when you use the vast power of consciousness to manifest a specific result. In other words, be careful what you visualize. You are going to get it.

With that little warning, I am now going to give you the secret of Alpha Picturing. It is a two-step method that I can tell you in a few seconds and which you can grasp intellectually even faster. But do not take it lightly. It is the most awesome secret ever withheld from mankind.

1. Relax very deeply.
2. Image assuredly.

If you were to do this now and, say, imaged somebody you wanted to telephone you, you would probably have to do it a number of times, possibly even over a period of days, before that telephone would ring. Eventually, it would, without a doubt.

However, if you were to do this after you have read a few more chapters, learning a number of techniques for deep relaxation, and practicing imaging in the way described, the telephone is going to ring much sooner, with your friend on the wire wondering why he or she called.

It takes practiced relaxation and practiced imaging to make dollars flow, locate lost objects, identify guilty parties, protect yourself from psychic attack, and compel others to act as you want them to act.

Relaxation can be very much deeper than you realize now.

Imaging can be very much more vivid and real than you realize at this point on your path to being a metaphysical miracle worker.

How to Use These
Steps to Improve Your Luck

"Show me," say my students at the University of Hawaii.

So I show them. And I am going to show you.

I am going to show you how to change your luck for the better without your having to read any further than this page.

Later you can work with more confidence in love, job, family, money, travel, cash, power, fame, and possessions.

Everybody can use better luck. Relax in this special way. Visualize in this special way. Read the steps through. Then do it.

Metaphysical
Action Plan
for
Better
Luck

1. Sit in a straight back chair.

2. Sigh deeply as you do when you let go at the end of the day.

3. Close your eyes and count backward slowly from 5 to 1.

4. Take another deep breath and as you exhale feel yourself relaxing even deeper.

5. Pretend you are at a carnival. You see the name as you enter "Carnival of Life."

6. You win at the penny pitching, at the numbers games, at everything you try.

7. You look at the date on a nearby calendar. It reads tomorrow's date.

8. You leave the carnival loaded with lucky prizes and notice the sign again as you leave "Carnival of Life."

9. Count forward from 1 to 5, commanding yourself to be fully alert at the count of 5.

If you want to improve your luck, do this metaphysical work now. Let me ask you some questions after you have completed the project:

A. Were you able to get over the initial strangeness of putting the book down and following these instructions?

B. Did you feel really tranquil?

C. Did counting backwards give you a feeling of descending even deeper into a state of relaxation?

D. Were you able to picture the carnival entrance gate and the "Carnival of Life" sign?

E. Did you feel confident walking up to the counter and putting your money down?

F. Were you able to visualize the wheel with the numbers spinning?

G. Did you select your prize or was it just handed to you?

Answer these questions to yourself before reading further. They contain the key to improving your success. Now let me give you these keys:

A. It is natural to feel strange at first. Few of us ever sit relaxed like this. We are always on the go. But the feeling of strangeness interferes with the quality of your tranquility. You need to practice on this and the next metaphysical projects until you feel totally comfortable in doing it.

B. If you did not feel strange, fine. But you still might not have been really relaxed. A true feeling of relaxation is a feeling of euphoria, of bliss. Some even feel ecstasy. Seek this delightful feeling more and more earnestly as you progress.

C. Counting backward is a popular technique. It should give you a feeling of descending into a deeper state of tranquility. If it doesn't, try imagining you are in an elevator going down—that is, if you are comfortable being in an elevator.

D. Picturing as if you are really there is the key to successful metaphysics. You are there. You see the sights. You smell the smells. You hear the sounds.

E. This is a critical point. No expectation of good luck, no good luck. <u>Expect it.</u> Know it will happen. After all, you are creating the scene, so you know you are going to be lucky.

F. This is a typical detail that signals reality in your visualizing. Image as if it were happening, and it does.

G. What matters is that you accepted it. Some people cannot accept good luck, so they don't manifest it in their life. It would be better to select your prize than to just accept the one handed you. <u>You must be in control.</u>

In these seven comments, I have given you keys to improving your metaphysical performance. So even if you did not do this metaphysical work for yourself, read over these seven comments for your future benefit.

Some of you may never have been to a carnival, that is, the kind of carnival where you can play these so-called games of skill and win prizes. If this is so, then here are some alternative imaging techniques. Pick the one that fits most vividly into your past experience so you can visualize realistically. Then create the same kind of lucky scene.

Carnival alternatives:

- Finding money in the street.
- Getting a big batch of mail—all of it good news.
- Playing poker or some other card game and winning every hand.

If you pick any of these alternatives, always insert a title associated with life. For instance, the street where you find the money has a street sign "Street of Life." The mailman's cap says "Life's Messages." The backs of the playing cards read "Game of Life."

Also, always see a calendar with the next day's date on it. If you are doing this quite early in the day, it would be alright to make the calendar read that day's date. The purpose is to fix the flow of good luck in the stream of time.

A University student who did this metaphysical work found that exam questions, for weeks, were exactly on what she had studied.

A real estate salesman met somebody the very next day—the day he had on his mental calendar—who both listed a house for sale and bought a house through him.

Later you will use your visual imagery in a nonsymbolic way. What you "see" *will be so.* Meanwhile . . .

Give your good luck free rein to come in any form. It's already on the way.

How to Use Your Mind
to Relax Your Body and Enhance Your Power

Something happens to your body when you relax your mind. Biofeedback devices record changes in cardiac output, blood lactate, and galvanic skin response.

Various meditative disciplines—yoga, self-hypnosis—all cause measurable body changes merely by holding the mind on some imaginary passive scene of some high spiritual concept.

You have already used your mind to relax your body in the metaphysical work you did for good luck. You imagined it was the end of the day when you sighed deeply. You counted backwards from 5 to 1. Perhaps you visualized an elevator descending with the numbers.

There are other ways to use the mind to relax the body—so many other ways that there are schools of meditation in India where you can spend a year or two just learning how to quiet the mind and relax the body.

Don't think that this means it is different. Theirs is the old school. We in the West have started from scratch and built a faster methodology.

Well, you say, I get there twice a day—on my way to sleep and again waking up. But there are two reasons why these moments are metaphysically useless: (1) You are not aware, or in control; (2) you slip in or out of sleep.

Deep relaxation is an aware state. You hear sounds quite sensitively. You are even more aware than you are right now. Here's why.

Measuring brain waves as a person relaxes, scientists find that the pulsations drop from an average of 14 to 21 for the active awake state to 7 to 14 for the relaxed awake state, then to about 4 to 7 just before sleep and 1 to 4 while asleep. These states are called beta, alpha, theta, and delta, just for quick identification.

A strange thing happens when we are asleep. When dreaming begins, the mind returns to the alpha state. When the dream is over, it goes again to the delta level.

The alpha state is the metaphysical state. There the mind can transcend time and space. People become psychic at the alpha state. They see into the future, through walls, over long distances and into the past.

You are about to learn how to reach the alpha level and do these things, too. If I am any sort of a teacher, you will get there, because it is the easiest thing you ever learned to do.

In the good luck work you did, you worked on your own consciousness. Most of us are not ready for good luck. A consciousness of unreadiness acts as a deterrent. In effect, we block normal good fortune by not being ready for it. So, by doing the carnival work, we change our own consciousness and permit good luck to flow through us.

There is much metaphysical work that we do on ourselves to perform miracles in our life. But the separation between ourselves and the next person is an illusion. It is almost as easy to enter his consciousness and invite changes as it is our own.

This is where the alpha relaxation comes in. And the realistic picturing, Alpha Picturing.

The following demonstration was made in front of a group of people. I gave one woman a list of mental pictures. She and another woman went to their alpha levels. The first woman held the first mental picture in her mind while the second woman called out what she saw: "A tree." It was correct. Then the next, "A horse." That was correct. They went through eleven pictures before an error occurred.

The alpha level of mind is the metaphysical level of mind. Here is how to experience it.

Metaphysical Action Plan for Alpha Picturing

1. Sit in a straight back chair. (Do not cross arms or legs.)

2. Take a deep breath and exhale your tensions.

3. Count backward from 5 to 1.

4. Take another deep breath and feel yourself becoming quite tranquil.

5. Visualize yourself in a beautiful flower garden.

6. Walk up to a blossom, smell the fragrance, see the texture of the petals, the swirling colors.

7. Notice one drop of water sparkling in the sun, like a diamond; all the colors of the rainbow appear in that one drop of water.

8. Lie down in the grass near the shrub and pretend you are falling asleep.

9. Imagine you are dreaming. You are able to reach anywhere as if you were a giant and the world was tiny.

10. Awake from your dreams and end your metaphysical work by telling yourself you will feel great at the count of five. "One, two, three, four, five!"

The Greatest Metaphysical Miracle: How to Become a Successful Metaphysician in One-Half Hour

If I were to tell you that you just inherited a fortune, but that you would have to take a few hours off today to sign papers and do whatever else was necessary to collect it, would you take the time off? Of course, you would. Well, that's just about where you stand right now. You cannot just read this book and become a miracle-making metaphysician. You have to put the book down and Alpha Picture in special ways. In other words, you have to *do* it to *be* it.

I have perfected a way for beginners to do less and still be it. You need not go anywhere or sign anything, but the fortune is still yours—a fortune in luxuries, friends, recognition, cash, and good health.

Here is what you have to do for one-half hour. It need not be uninterrupted. You can do it in three 10 minute periods if you wish, but they should be within a 24-hour period. Repeat the following project six times:
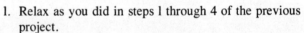

Metaphysical Action Plan for Making Alpha Picturing Effective

1. Relax as you did in steps 1 through 4 of the previous project.

2. Experience the flower garden as you did in steps 5 through 7.

3. Visualize a scene of the past. (See explanation below.)

4. Visualize a scene in the future. (See explanation below.)

5. Visualize a scene taking place now but at a great distance away. (See explanation below.)

6. End by saying, "Next time I will relax deeper, and visualize even better. I feel wide awake and great at the count of five. One, two, three, four, five!"

Let me give some detailed instructions for steps 3, 4, and 5.

Explanation of 3: Daydream about your first day of school. Where was it? How old were you? Who went with you? How did you get there? What was your teacher like? Or, pick an event like your last moving day, going through all the details, especially your last look at the old place. Or daydream about how you met somebody special.

Explanation of 4: Select tomorrow, or next New Year's Eve or your birthday three years from now. Let your mind just play a scene of that day in the future.

Explanation of 5: Do you have a relative that lives at a distance? The further the better, but even in the next town will do. What might that person be doing right now?

Each of these three visualizing steps need take no more than one minute. So, the whole project should take no more than five minutes. You can select the same event and repeat it, or different events—whatever you would enjoy doing.

This is where you cross the threshold between being a see it, hear it, touch it, smell it, taste it, "physical" person and becoming a beyond-space, beyond-time, mind-over-matter, "metaphysical" person.

Do it today. I'll wait . . . .

How to Test Yourself as a Metaphysician

"Was I really in Alpha?"

"Was I picturing clearly enough?"

These are two questions that plague beginners. I will wager you were doing fine. Oh, you could probably do better, and you will do better. But right now it does not matter because you are going to create small miracles in your life first, then larger miracles. If you have spent that half hour, you are able to go deep enough in Alpha and visualize well enough to create a car for yourself, or get rid of that pain, or attract that person to you.

Later, you will feel reinforced by these smaller miracles and be able to go in to the bigger miracles. Your metaphysical power grows with each success.

But . . .Those two questions that lurk in your mind now need to be answered. Are you really in Alpha? Are you picturing realistically? I want to put your mind at ease, because doubt interferes even with small miracles.

Here are two tests you can do. One confirms whether or not you were at Alpha. The other confirms whether or not you are picturing realistically.

Let me explain the Alpha test. Of course, the only real test for Alpha is a biofeedback device that measures brain pulsations and signals either with a light or buzzer when you are there. These are expensive. There is an effective alternative that uses your own subconscious mind as a biofeedback device.

A popular system for measuring the depth of relaxation was devised for hypnotists. It is called the Le Cron-Bordeaux system after its inventors. It spells out 50 levels as evidenced by physiological changes. I have reduced these to 10 levels and paraphrase them below. You do not need to memorize these. All you need to do is read them slowly, understanding them. Do this now, and then I will tell you what to do next to complete the Alpha test.

Ten Levels of Relaxation

1. Physical Comfort.
2. Eyes closed.
3. Mind stops flitting from here to there.
4. Physical comfort increases to lethargy—no desire to move.
5. Breathing slows down, becomes deeper.
6. Feeling of heaviness from head to foot.
7. Feeling of detachment from surroundings.
8. Feeling like in a trance-like state.
9. Ability to create analgesia in hand.
10. Ability to open eyes without affecting relaxation.

After you read this list, here is what you should do. This is the first test:

A. Relax and go to the flower garden.
B. Ask your mind to have a number from 1 to 10 pop into your mind as soon as you end your session on the count of 5, indicating just how deep you were.
C. End your session as you usually do and wait for a number to pop into your mind.

Any number of four or more is indicative of the Alpha state. If you have a number come to mind and it is four or more, you are ready for the second test.

This next test is for picturing. Read it through first and then do it. Here is your second test:

A. Relax.

B. Imagine a bucket of ice water beside you on the right side of your chair. Place your right hand in this ice water. Feel the ice cubes against your hand.

C. Hold your hand in the imaginary ice water, knowing it is getting more and more numb.

D. After about five minutes, tell yourself the following: "In a moment I am going to open my eyes and pinch my numb right hand. It will not disturb my alpha level. I will remain relaxed. I will also pinch my left hand to feel the difference. I will then restore feeling to my right hand by merely saying 'hand normal' and I will feel by pinching it that full feeling has been restored."

E. Open your eyes. Test your right hand. Then compare to the left hand. Say "hand normal" and test again. If necessary, repeat "hand normal" until feeling is fully restored.

F. End your session in the usual way.

Getting Rid of Pain
—A Quick Metaphysical Reward

How would you like to be able to get rid of pain in any part of your body at will?

Well, if you have passed these two tests, you can. Here is how.

The numbness you have created in your hand is transferable. You heard me right. You can actually touch any painful part of your body, like your forehead or lower back or knee and have the numbness leave your hand and enter the painful area, by just telling it to.

Now, pain is an important symptom. It is nature's way of saying that something is not what it should be. Don't feel you can use this as a permanent pain killer. Let me put it more succinctly:

Warning! Create numbness in a pained area only for temporary relief. If pain persists, see your doctor.

It is good to repeat test number two a few times so that the process becomes quicker and even more effective. Then when pain strikes, you need only to relax, picture your hand in a bucket of ice water and it is numb.

Mrs. N.E., a real estate agent, had constant headaches. Her doctor called them migraine. Aspirins upset her stomach. Similar pain relieving medication dulled her senses. After years of suffering, she was taught this technique. It gave her immediate relief whenever she used it.

A woman was in an automobile accident. She was thrown clear of the car as it swerved and overturned. Even before passers-by got to her, she had passed numbness from her hand to her right shin where there was a compound fracture and to other parts of her body where there were painful gravel burns and bruises. In this way, she reduced the effects of shock and maintained her composure. She actually joked with the ambulance crew when they arrived.

Stopping pain may not be a miracle. But it certainly can be a rewarding skill to have.

Passing test number one and test number two insures that you are capable of miracles.

In the next chapter, you begin to make them happen.

3

How to Create a Miracle in Your Life Today

Do you know that your mental pictures are "real" enough to affect photographic film? I have read about Ted Serios, the man who could do this at will, but I personally witnessed three people who on separate occasions have obtained clear pictures their very first try. The procedure is to use a Polaroid camera for instant developing (some have been successful using light sensitive paper without a camera).

Hold the camera up to the head of the person in a pitch dark room or closet. When the person relaxes and images, he says, "Now," and you snap.

A man, who lived on a boat, visualized his mooring. Sure enough, there was the row of boats alongside a pier. A girl visualized the moon over the ocean. It came out, reflection and all. A young man who visualized a face produced it.

Does this give you an idea of how *real* your mental images are and how they can affect matter?

You can influence the throw of dice, the roulette wheel, the slot machine—if that is your goal. I, myself, prefer to shoot for more meaningful benefits like "bumping in" to the right person who can use my talents; moving a car for a parking spot in the right place when I need it; or influencing a decision in my favor. How would you like to use the power of your mental images? In this chapter, you get a giant step closer to doing it.

The Miracles Get
Bigger and Bigger, Better and Better

Some people are not miracle makers. Other people are. Those who are not are the people who say, "I can't." Those who are miracle makers are the people who say, "I can."

This should not surprise you. It works the same for whatever we do in life—or do not do.

If you know you cannot ride a bicycle, you do not stay balanced for more than a couple of seconds. I am sure you have taught children to ride bicycles, and some adults, the same way I have: You hold them and walk or trot alongside of them. Then they find out later you weren't holding them, and they realize they can do it by themselves.

I have taught adult writing classes. What do I teach? Certainly not how to put words together. I spend 90 percent of the time convincing them that if they can talk, they can write. Next thing I know, they are published.

In the case of affecting photographic film with their thoughts, remember I said "their very first try." If it does not happen on the first try with somebody, or yourself, don't waste any more film.

On the first try you have hope, expectation and at least some measure of "I can." When the picture turns out black without any light forms on it at all, the "I can" diminishes. It moves closer to "I can't" and also the level of hope and expectation drops. If there was not enough hope, expectation, and "I can" the first time, there is certainly not going to be enough the second time, and still less the third.

That is one reason why I have to start you off on small miracles, the ones that happen easiest and quickest. I cannot risk your failure. Once your face gets grim and you say, "It didn't happen; I can't," it becomes a rougher path to hoe.

On the other hand, once your mouth opens in astonishment and joy and you exclaim, "I did it! I can!" then the way is paved for bigger and better miracles.

Then pretty soon you graduate as a full fledged metaphysician.

How to Acquire Metaphysical Power
That You Can Focus Like a Laser Beam

Stories are still told how, in the early thirteenth century, Francis of Assisi, who was later made a saint, attracted birds to him and other friendly wild animals. These birds and animals treated him as if he were one of them.

St. Francis was "in" on a metaphysical secret. He gave this secret to the world, but did not label it as "secret for accomplishing metaphysical miracles," so the world labeled his teachings as just another set of religious niceties.

Here is the secret as St. Francis stated it: It is better to pardon than to be pardoned. It is better to love than to be loved. It is better to give than to receive.

Let me put this in the metaphysical language for you: Power flows through a pipe, but not through a receptacle.

The best way to tap into a flow of this miraculous life energy is to make a pipe out of yourself at first. That is, create a miracle or two for your spouse, or a member of your family, or a friend. You are then developing yourself as a channel for the flow of this energy in any direction you wish to focus it—including your own personal miracles.

Francis of Assisi did such loving things as give all his wealth to a leper he passed in the street. It was a miracle for the leper but it caused such metaphysical energy to flow through Francis that animals felt its power and miracle after miracle followed.

Khalil Gibran, author of *The Prophet,* put it this way:

> Do not invite rich people to your house for dinner. You will be repaid by their inviting you to their house for dinner. Invite poor people to your house for dinner. They cannot repay you, so the universe must repay you.
>
> When the universe repays you . . . expect a miracle.

Some of you may think I am getting "religious" on you. Actually I am still talking about that same energy that you felt with your own hands earlier in this book. It is a life energy that fills space. Most of us live in this energy and are not aware of it. When we become aware of this energy, we are in effect sending up an antenna to receive it and harness it, pretty much as we did, eventually, with electrical energy.

Occasionally a man becomes aware of this life energy that surrounds him. He sees that it flows through him in vaster ways the moment he becomes conscious of it. He sees that it flows even more abundantly through him when he directs it toward the growth and survival of life in general. He tries to explain this to others. But what do they do? They just build a church around him.

A medical physician I know is also a metaphysician. Here is what he occasionally does in the course of an office visit. He relaxes and says to himself, "I feel one with the power that surrounds me."

Instantly, the patient seems to feel a rapport and relaxes, too. That alone begins a cure, but it also permits the physician's "healthy image" to enter the patient's subconscious, which controls the body. The cure is accelerated and there are frequently very dramatic changes in that single office visit.

Can you feel part of a power bigger than you are? If you can, your conscious mind is able to focus that power the way a magnifying glass focuses the sun's rays. If you can see past the illusion of separate heads, separate consciousnesses, and into the reality of a greater consciousness that we all share, you are then able to focus the power of that greater consciousness.

You know that the bigger the magnifying glass, the more of the sun's rays it can gather in, and the quicker what those rays are focused on begins to smoulder and catch fire.

You can focus the energy of greater consciousness into a laser-like beam that you can put to work for you in many different ways.

A One Minute Mental Trip
That Magnifies Your Power a Hundredfold

Suspecting that you are part of this greater consciousness is not enough.

The late Walter Russell was able to harness this energy of universal consciousness to create in many different directions. He was a registered architect with a number of buildings to his credit. He was a physicist and co-discoverer of heavy water, precursor to the atomic age. He sculpted three presidents. He was a poet, author, philosopher, composer, and teacher. His biographer called him "The Man Who Tapped the Secrets of the Universe."

When I met Walter Russell over a decade ago, I remarked, "You must have tremendous faith."

He replied, "I have no faith. I know."

You, too, must *know*. You must know you are part of this energy of a greater consciousness. Suspecting that this might be so makes you a very weak magnifying glass, indeed; so weak, you better find a boy scout to rub two sticks together to start that fire for you. Believing with a grain of salt, like, "I'll take your word for it for the time being," is not enough either. Understanding the concept as an outside observer will not do it either. You have to *be* part of this larger energy in order to focus it like a laser beam.

You are. But you separate yourself because you see your body as separate; you know your thoughts are secluded so you see your consciousness as separate. That is why there are ordinary men, and extraordinary men called metaphysicians.

Sit for a moment and contemplate this concept. Notice the blocks in your acceptance of it. Reason them away. Then do this metaphysical work that reinforces your *knowing* you are part of a larger consciousness that surrounds you.

Metaphysical Action Plan for Gathering In Power

1. Relax as before.
2. "See" a sphere of light around you. It is the energy of your consciousness.
3. "See" it expand and fill the room you are in, then all the rooms in your home.
4. "See" it spread over the town you live in, the state, the whole country.
5. Your light now envelops the planet earth. Send it out even further to encompass the solar system, the entire galaxy, other galaxies.
6. Now gradually bring this sphere of light back to this galaxy, this solar system, this planet, this country, this room.
7. Send your consciousness now to the center of the sphere of light, deep within you.
8. Repeat, "Universal energy surges through me as I go forth!"
9. End, feeling great, at the count of five.

Congratulations! You Are a Metaphysician—Prove It to Yourself Now by Transforming an Enemy into a Friend

She had lived with him for two months. That morning they had another of their succession of fights. He figured it was the end. Sure enough, when he returned from work, she had packed and left. An expensive dress he had bought her was torn to shreds and lay on the floor. To show her animosity, she emptied flour, salt, and sugar all over the floor of the apartment.

He was beside himself. He decided to "patch things up" metaphysically. He relaxed and pictured her. He sent apologies and surrounded her mentally with love and support. Within an hour, she returned and helped him clean the floor.

If you have done the metaphysical work set forth so far in this book—especially the six five-minute sessions—and passed the two tests in Chapter 12 . . .

If you have done this metaphysical project of expanding your consciousness to embrace the galaxies, and accepting the flow of universal energy through you . . .

Then, congratulations, you are a metaphysician, able to make changes in your life. If I could, I would hand you a diploma.

Remember, earlier in this chapter, I explained how this energy that you are now channeling through you flows through a pipe a lot more freely than through a receptacle. This means you have to use this energy, not just let it sit. You need to use it to help others, not just keep it within yourself.

Here is an idea! Why not help others to help you? You can do this right now. You can prove to yourself that you deserve that imaginary diploma. Here is how.

Pick somebody in your life who is giving you a hard time. Is there somebody in your family—a child or a parent, a sister or a brother—who is obstinate, unreasonable, disrespectful?

Pick somebody that you would like to have become less of a problem to you. Do the following metaphysical work. Then watch a change take place within 24 hours!

Metaphysical Action Plan to Transform the Bad in a Person to Good

1. Relax in the usual way.

2. See the person in front of you. The facial expression is negative. The posture is typically hostile.

3. See yourself surrounded in light. It is the sphere of your awareness or consciousness. Make the light brighter. It is so bright it feels warm now. It is a good feeling.

4. Expand the sphere of light so that it envelopes the other person, too. See the facial expression and posture change as the light reaches him or her.

5. Say mentally, "Your attitude is not my problem. Why not change it? You will feel better. We can work together effectively."

6. Feel a warmth between you. See yourselves shake hands or embrace.

> 7. Restore your light so that it again surrounds you, re-
> duce its brightness and end your session in the usual
> way.

If you do this metaphysical work just once, it will have an obvious effect. The next time you see this person there will be a noticeable difference in attitude toward you.

Do it three times for a really dramatic result. Spread the repetitions over a period of days, preferably after seeing the person.

How to Make Friends out of
Enemies and Win Support from Opponents

You are not limited to one person. As soon as you see the astonishing changes that take place, you can use this same metaphysical project to improve relations with:

- A troublesome teenager.
- A malicious gossip.
- A noisy neighbor.
- An obstructionist to social or cultural projects.
- An unethical competitor.
- An unpleasant co-worker.

A woman who lived in a suburban development was spreading unkind rumors about another woman's daughter. She kept telling people that the daughter was flirting with the married men in the area. Since the daughter was going steady with a young man, her mother knew it was the woman's jealousy or some other such problem.

She did the metaphysical work described above. The gossiping stopped and about a week later the woman brought them a loaf of bread she had baked.

You can get results with anybody who is "bugging" you. You can add special ingredients to your light. So far we have called the light "warm" and "good." The most powerful ingredient you can add is love.

It is not easy to send love to an old grouch or a young brat. If you can crank it up, you will find it well worth the effort. After all, that power that surrounds and surges through you surrounds the grouch or brat, too.

But if love is too far for you to go at this moment, try giving your light such qualities as:

- Understanding
- Empathy
- Oneness
- Rapport
- Harmony
- Peace

Later, I am going to provide you with the metaphysical "recipe" to affect whole groups of people. Can you imagine the possibilities? You can work on elections. You can work on your customers. You can work on people who are not your customers who ought to be your customers. You can work on the people of another country. You can help to improve the consciousness of people everywhere on earth.

You Can Even Make Changes in Cats or Dogs and Get Rid of Invading Insects

A woman who attended one of my metaphysical classes practiced by "seeing" her dog in her light. When she returned home, the dog was especially affectionate in greeting her and remained so all evening.

A man named Boone wrote a book called *Kinship with All Life*,[1] in which he told how he trained Strong Heart, a dog who later became famous in silent film days.

The rapport between trainer and dog did not happen right away. In fact, the dog seemed to resist all efforts of the trainer. Then one late afternoon, Boone sat down to watch a sunset. The dog sat, quietly observing it, too. Boone felt love for the dog.

Then a change took place. From that moment on, the dog cooperated fully and later became a star. Boone went on to use his method of love to create bridges of friendship with other animals—wild horses, snakes, and even a common housefly.

It is hard to feel love. Even happy marriages find that expressions of love do not flow that easily. Some parents die without their children ever having said they love them.

[1] J. Allen Boone, *Kinship with All Life*, (New York, N.Y.: Harper and Row, 1954).

If it is so hard to feel love for other people, how can one possibly feel love for animals, and even insects? The answer is you probably cannot. But if you understand that all life is the same energy of consciousness expressing in different ways, then you have a beginning.

Boone found that if you looked down on an animal as beneath you, there was no rapport. Communication developed only when you saw the other form of life as an equal.

I used this principle to get rid of small red ants that decided to share my house on Long Island without sharing the mortgage payments or tax bills. I relaxed. I "saw" them and had a friendly talk with them. I bargained with them as I would with an equal. "You don't belong in the house. Leave the house and you may stay on the property." I surrounded them in understanding light. They left.

The trouble with working with insects like this is that the attractive force that brought in one colony can bring in another. Also, the generation span is so brief, a whole new group can be on your doorstep again in a few weeks. Then, back you must go to repeat your metaphysical work.

Alpha Picturing Takes Your Consciousness Any Place You Want It to Go

When you picture an obstinate person and make changes by surrounding him in your light, your consciousness actually goes to that person.

Experiments with mental telepathy show that thought travels instantly over thousands of miles. When you imagine that your light reaches around the earth, it does. When you imagine that your light goes out beyond this galaxy, it does.

Before you finish this book, you will agree it does. But right now I want you to know that it moves out a mile or a hundred miles.

Do this test:

Metaphysical Action Plan for Traveling in Consciousness

1. Go to a spot near your bed. Examine the wall. Notice every fly speck, every detail of paint, wallpaper, or woodwork. Memorize it so you can recall it.

2. Do the same with two more spots, each a step further away into the hall or another room.

3. Now lie on your bed, in the usual deep way; relax and visualize spot #1, then spot #2, then spot #3, seeing again all those details.

4. Now visualize spot #4, further away, that you did not visit and memorize. Check out all its details.

5. End your relaxation in the usual way. Then get up and visit those three spots to see how well you did.

6. Now visit that spot #4. How did you do? Are the tiny details as you saw them?

If you were able to see spot #4 almost as well as the spots you previously visited and memorized, it should be convincing proof that you traveled at least a few feet without your body.

We do this all the time. We do this in dreams. We do it in daydreams. Then the phone rings. "That's funny. I was just thinking of you."

How to See Through
Walls and over Great Distances

Over 70 colleges in the United States now offer courses in parapsychology and ESP (extrasensory perception). New and more accurate ways are being devised to test ESP phenomena, including the phenomenon known as clairvoyance—the ability to see events when you are not present to see them visually.

Out-of-body experiences are getting a lot of scientific attention. Once the strictly hearsay legends of India and Africa where a person was frequently said to have been seen in two places at the same time, these out-of-body experiences are being investigated at American centers with startling results.

A person who claims that his mind has left his body and goes to another location is able to provide information that is checked out and found to be accurate. Also, researchers have come upon instances where people so "visited" have reported they saw the person at that precise time and place, or have felt the presence of that person.

I know a psychiatrist who made a study of this ten years ago, but her findings were too "far out," she felt, at that time to discuss professionally. So she wrote a novel about industrial espionage being carried out by such out-of-body methods. I don't know if it was ever published.

She was able, however, to discuss professionally another phenomenon: Patients, while free associating on her office couch, would frequently describe events that took place in her own life.

"I see a yellow plate breaking on the floor. Somebody says, 'Be careful, don't cut yourself!' "

This had happened a few hours previously in the psychiatrist's own kitchen. By tabulating such events, she found it happened most frequently with patients who were repressed, not too communicative, and also with patients with whom she had developed a closer rapport.

She had her findings published in a professional journal and later received confirmation from other psychiatrists, who, up until then, were too intimidated by the implications of this phenomenon to talk about it.

How do you control this ability? How do you send your mind out to see whom you wish to see? How do you retrieve needed information one thousand or more miles away? A few sensitive psychics have proven this to be possible. But for most people it has been happening only as a spontaneous experience.

You already know the two most important steps to accomplish this: (1) Going to the alpha level of mind; (2) using your visualizing faculty.

A noted psychic in Phoenix wanted to impress a young woman with his ability. He went to his alpha level, pictured her and then observed the picture. She was in bed reading a book. He noted the title. There was an astrological mural on the wall. He made a mental note of details.

The next morning he phoned her, told her at what time she had been reading in bed, the name of the book, and what he liked about the mural. Needless to say, he made an impression!

Small miracles first. Step by step. Do this yourself tonight, but on a smaller scale. Later, you can try your mental wings on longer trips.

When you are ready to retire tonight, check out somebody in your home. That person can be in the next room or elsewhere in the house or apartment. Here is how:

Metaphysical Action Plan to See Through Walls

1. Relax very deeply as you have learned to do.
2. Go to the flower garden and review the beauty, the scents, the drop of water.
3. Now visualize the room where the person is whom you are checking out.
4. "Be" there. Accept whatever you "see." Do not *try* to see. Just let it happen.
5. End your session feeling great at the count of five!

Now, investigate discreetly how accurate you were. It is best not to divulge to the person exactly what you were testing. Some people are not ready to cope with such concepts.

Mark well in your mind where you were correct. Dismiss for now any inaccuracies in what you may have detected. Accuracy improves each time you perform in this metaphysical manner.

Expand Your Consciousness
As You Stretch Your Mind

It is just as easy to check out somebody a thousand miles away as it is to see through a wall into the next room. There is no traveling involved. It is not like so-called soul travel or astral travel. Your consciousness is instantly there. Later I will share with you some metaphysical techniques that will simplify the procedure and up your batting average.

I remember one metaphysical class I was attending years ago. A young student just could not believe he could do it. "I can't visualize that well," he said to the teacher.

"Stand up," ordered the teacher as he moved toward the back of the classroom where this young man was seated. "Now before I reach you I want you to tell me this woman's problem." The teacher held a card in his hand and read off the woman's name, age, and address—some 3,000 miles away.

Without thinking, the young man rattled off that she had lost her left arm from the elbow and had a circulation problem. He finished just as the teacher reached him and handed him the card. His face lit up. He was absolutely right.

He could—as long as he did not have time to worry about it.

Everybody can, if they can get the reasoning intellect out of their way.

You can, and will, providing . . .

This book is a metaphysical program. Step by step you develop your metaphysical ability. If you dive ahead into a metaphysical project without having taken the necessary training of previous action steps, you fail. Then, failure convinces you that you cannot. And, the conviction that you cannot places you right back with all those people who do not believe in metaphysics and so never experience it.

Take the steps. Do the projects already described in these three chapters. True, they are only small miracles. But you need the training.

And . . . they get better and better.

4

How to Expand Your Power as a Metaphysician to Win Life's Really Big Prizes

Many scientists today are taking a second look at metaphysical phenomena. Where, ten years ago, they would not be caught with a person claiming psychic ability, today they vie for the privilege of studying such people.

Psychologist Lawrence Le Shan has been studying people with healing power for a number of years. In the process, he has seen the strangest phenomena happen too many times to ignore. He considers the problem to be with our accepted scientific framework.

Science needs to change, he says, to explain and accept the unexplainable. And he makes a commendable start in his book, *The Medium, the Mystic, and the Physicist,* [1] where he points in the general direction of a general theory explaining the paranormal.

Le Shan runs a course designed to bring out the healing power in people. A national magazine recently reported on this course and the success of one of his pupils, Maria Janis, daughter of Gary Cooper and wife of pianist Byron Janis. Mrs. Janis has performed a number of metaphysical healings and has been called in by several hospitals to assist patients who are not responding to treatment.

The key to this Le Shan course is quieting the body and the mind. Sound familiar? This going into the alpha level of mind is the key to metaphysical powers.

[1] Lawrence Le Shan, *The Medium, the Mystic and the Physicist,* (New York, N.Y.: Viking Press, Inc., 1974).

Intelligent people are often able to scan a book in an hour or less and gain some insight as to its scope and content. However, the person who is not yet a metaphysician can never become a metaphysician by merely flipping through the pages or even reading slowly.

To become a metaphysician, you must experience the relaxation of body. You must experience the relaxation of mind. You must experience mental pictures so that you are thoroughly at home with them. You must begin by making small changes in your own luck, or in other people, before you can go on to bigger changes.

This is the step-by-step process set forth in the first three chapters. Your handling of these three chapters determines your future as a metaphysician.

Let me give it to you straight: The top column leads to the bottom column . . . .

If You Experience

Deeper and deeper body relaxation,
More and more tranquil mind relaxation,
Clearer and clearer imaging,
Your ability to create hand numbness,
Your changing your own luck,
Your making changes in other people,
Sending your consciousness out of your body,

Then You Can

Improve your health.
Accelerate your success.
Influence other people.
Attract the opposite sex.
Create a flow of money.
See ahead in time.
Know what is happening anywhere.

How to Get Lady Luck
to Work Full Time for You

I promised you that if you are willing to perform small miracles first, you will be able to go on to bigger and better miracles. In an earlier chapter, you practiced Alpha Picturing to change your luck in a general sort of way with the winning at a carnival imaging. Let's take another look at luck and proceed to give it a real boost.

I was about to say, "beyond your belief,"—a typical superlative. But this would be inaccurate. It can only be as great an improvement as your belief will permit.

You are now a few steps ahead in your belief. So you create bigger and better—to a degree. Then, as you see the results, you will be able to accept—and perform—bigger and better miracles. One day, you will feel that anything is possible. And you will be right.

Not too long ago, you would not get many psychologists to talk about luck. Now they pretty much agree that luck is influenced by our state of mind. I'll let you in on a secret. These psychologists are still talking about luck from a rather limited view. They see unlucky people as accident-prone people. They see unlucky people as pessimistic people. They see unlucky people as people with a lack of self-confidence.

So they say, sure luck is affected by your state of mind. The person with an unconscious desire to inflict self-punishment has a number of unlucky accidents. The person who feels the world is against him invites opposition. The person who has no confidence in himself makes unlucky mistakes.

But you and I know that luck can be measured over a wider parameter than that. As consciousness joins consciousness as part of a greater consciousness, individual luck transcends the psychology of the individual and involves a greater psyche.

Shall we call that psyche Lady Luck?

Lady Luck has her limits. She does not have dominion over certain events that are out of her jurisdiction. For instance, a man prayed for a million dollars and got it the next day. The man was Reverend Frank Gunsaulus, pastor of Chicago's Plymouth Congregational Church. He wanted to start a new technical college based on advanced educational precepts. He needed a million dollars.

One Saturday afternoon he decided to inform the newspapers that his Sunday sermon would be titled "What I Would Do if I Had a Million Dollars." On Sunday morning, he knelt and prayed for that million. The church was well attended. When the sermon was over, a man approached the pulpit and offered the million. He was Philip Armour, head of the meat packing firm. And so was born what is today the Illinois Institute of Technology.

No, that was not luck. I'll wager Lady Luck let her Boss handle that one.

Lady Luck still parcels out a lot of loot. If she is not handing out money, she's handing out green lights, lottery tickets that win, and just the right amount of breeze to make that hit a home run.

We are not ruling out receiving help from her Boss, but first things first. How do we get help from Lady Luck when we want it? Like all the time.

Most people do not give Lady Luck any room in their concept of life. They call it superstitious, childish, unscientific.

From what you now know about the energy of consciousness, it should be obvious to you that these people are cutting out one very helpful sector of the larger consciousness of which we are a part.

Make room for Lady Luck in your life, give her space, and she moves in!

The Three Levels of Good Fortune That You Can Now Claim

You can identify three basic souces of so-called luck:

1. Psychological stance.
2. Lucky happenstance.
3. Epic circumstance.

You need to work on all three levels to claim the good fortune that is rightfully yours. What does it avail the lucky poker player who is accident-prone and has to spend his winnings on medical care? What does it avail the lucky salesman with a series of record-breaking months if his firm goes bankrupt?

The stance of your personality must be positive (1). There must be space in your life for Lady Luck (2). You must be in tune with higher consciousness (3).

So you see the metaphysical work you have to do? It is in three stages. But even before you finish the second stage, there can be an outpouring of great good into your life.

Here is a true account of a few days in the life of a man who obviously needed to do some, if not all, of this metaphysical work to advantage. He is a wealthy contractor living in Hawaii. The following happened to him:

- A friend borrowed his yacht without permission, sailed it to another island, and broke the mast.
- He finished building his own dream house only to have it burn to the ground—estimated loss $250,000.

- He stumbled and broke a toe.
- His Mark IV stalled on the freeway and in the process of a tow truck hauling it away, it scraped against a concrete embankment and a side was ripped off.
- He bought a new wardrobe to replace the clothes he lost in the fire, took a trip to get away from his troubles, and the airline lost his luggage.

Misfortune can be on all of these three levels, too. A man came to me some ten years ago claiming he had a system to beat the races. he wanted me to help him write a book about it. It was a good system. It exploited the cycles that take place in a person's luck, betting less and less as you lost, more and more as you won. I never wrote the book but I certainly could endorse the validity of his premise.

Pit one random computer against another random computer: You find that the incidence of "hits" of one computer "guessing" the other do not run in cycles. It sticks fairly close to statistical predictions. Statistics can predict even the probable deviation from strict averages.

But pit a man against a computer spewing out random numbers and you get quite a different story. There are usually wider deviations from the statistical predictions and longer cycles of being right and being wrong.

What factor enters the picture? Man's consciousness, of course.

How to Get Out of Your
Own Way and Permit Good Luck to Flow

I am going to ask you to do three metaphysical projects to start an incredible flow of good fortune into your life.

The first will correct psychological blocks which interfere with good luck and which even invite bad luck.

The second will make room in your life for outside support—call that support Dame Fortune or Lady Luck, if you wish.

The third will attune your consciousness to the universal consciousness from where the really big rewards emanate.

You will be asked to do these three metaphysical projects just once. But use your own discretion as to whether reinforcement in one of these might be necessary in your case. Some people need a lot of psychological alignment, others more alignment with universal consciousness.

The great thing about these three metaphysical projects is that though they are directed at good luck and good fortune, they pave the way even further for miracle making success in the chapters that follow.

Here are the five main psychological blocks that invite bad luck in place of good luck.

Anxiety and worry. This causes tension in the body. Muscle coordination and mental efficiency can be affected. Good health is interfered with—usually the digestive system is affected first, but hardly any part of the body is immune and symptoms range from headaches to heart attacks.

Fear. This is the most insidious block of all. Substitute fearlessness for fear and you change your life. Other people sense your fear; even animals can. You telegraph your fear. You become prey.

Self-hate. You heap blame on yourself. Or disdain. Or recrimination. You invite punishment subconsciously—some by overeating, overdrinking, or being excessive in other ways.

Pessimism. You have little expectation of success so you prove yourself right by failing. You have little hope for a bright tomorrow, so the world obliges.

Limited Self-Image. You don't think enough of yourself so you don't get enough out of life. Your limited self-image limits your accomplishments.

You are not performing true metaphysical magic by removing these blocks, but you cannot be an effective metaphysician until you do. Actually, psychologists and psychiatrists remove them for their clients and patients without any thought to metaphysics.

However, it is a time consuming process involving the identification of deep-seated causes and then prolonged reconditioning sessions.

The ancient Polynesian kahunas, or spiritual medicine men, were highly advanced metaphysicians. The metaphysical work you are about to do is startlingly effective. It is adapted from the kahunas. It takes less than three minutes. Do it now.

Metaphysical Action Plan for Getting Out of Your Own Way	1. Relax deeply in your usual way. 2. Be still for a minute or so, concentrating on your rhythmic breathing. 3. Speak to your subconscious mind. Order all anxiety, worry, fear, self-recrimination, pessimism, and other unwanted negative attitudes to prepare to leave your body.

4. Tell your subconscious mind that a moment or so after you end your session you will get up and shake first your right leg then your left leg and all of these negativities will leave you for good.

5. See yourself getting up, walking outside your home (preferably near the garbage area), shaking your legs in turn, and gray matter drifting down out of your body.

6. See yourself free of this negativity, standing erect, confident, capable, effective, and strong.

7. End your session.

8. Move outside and shake your right leg vigorously and then your left leg. Leave the immediate area.

9. Stand erect noticing how optimistic you feel, how courageous and confident.

One young man who was plagued with shyness did this exercise in one of my classes. He returned the following week smiling, talkative, outgoing. Everybody noticed the change in him when he arrived, but nobody, including myself, put two and two together until the end of the class, the time for comments and questions.

"I want to tell you what happened after the last class," he said. There was a hush. It was the first time this fellow had spoken up in class. "When I got out to the sidewalk, I shook my right leg, then my left leg. I didn't notice, but there was a young lady passing by who had stopped to watch. She asked me what I was doing. Ordinarily, I would have mumbled something and beat a hasty retreat. I told her of this class. We had coffee together. When I got home, I did it again. Next morning, I spoke up to my boss about a better way to do something. I thought he'd punch me. Instead, he gave me a raise. I've done the project a third time so I'm wondering what's going to happen next."

What escaped through this young man's shaking legs was his own shakiness about himself. His negative self-doubts ran out and a natural self-confidence took its place. He no longer stood in the way of his own good luck.

Make Room in Your Life for Great Happenings

The blocks are out of the pipeline. Now you can turn on the tap of good luck, and enjoy a flow of fortuituous happenings day after day.

Most people who are beset by things that keep going wrong are so busy with these problems and the unhappiness they bring, there is no room in their life for a change. When I say no room, I mean they fill their consciousness with their problems instead of dwelling on solutions and fortuitous happenings.

GOLDEN ✳ KEY

You may not be one of these people, but if I offered you an extra room in your house free of charge, would you refuse? Of course, not. Take a look around now and see where you would like this extra room to be located.

What you will be doing is making room for Lady Luck in your life. In a special way.

Metaphysical Action Plan for Making Space in Your Life for Good Luck

1. Relax deeply.

2. Picture yourself at the doorway of a new room just added to your house. All there is now are four walls, a ceiling, and a floor.

   ROOM

3. If you wish to make it larger, just push the walls back. If you'd like a higher ceiling, just raise it. Put windows in where you want them. Create a skylight in the ceiling. The moment you do, the room is filled with brilliant light.

   EXPAND SKYLIGHT

4. Paint and decorate, using bright colors. Furnish the room any way you wish—an armchair for yourself; a few other chairs or couch for others; curtains, carpet, or rugs.

   DECORATE FURNISH

5. Now place a cosmic computer in the room. It looks like a typewriter. Whatever you will later feed into the computer sets appropriate events in your life.

   computer

6. Put the finishing touches in this brilliant room. Then activate the computer by mentally typing your name and then the words "Good luck, channel open. Begin flow."

   TYPE NAME

7. End your session feeling great.

I will be telling you how to use this room in many beneficial ways. It is always there for you to enter. If you don't believe me, see for yourself. Go back there now and you will find everything just as you created it. In every single detail. All you do is:

Metaphysical Action Plan for Good Luck Reinforcement

1. Relax.
2. Be at the doorway, then enter.
3. Look around.

4. Walk up to the good luck computer again; type your name and the words, "Good luck channel open. Increase flow."

5. End your session, feeling great.

How to Put Your Hat in the Ring for the Really Big Rewards

First you cleared out the negative blocks that were standing in the way of your good luck. Next you created room in your life for good things to happen. Now you are ready for the big prizes. You become eligible for these by a metaphysical act known as tuning in.

We are no longer talking about luck. We are talking about the really big turn of events that "makes" you.

A public relations man in his early forties was just scraping by. It was tough going to get newspapers to accept stories about his restaurant clients and other commercial ventures that he was paid to get publicity for. He found he had to pull off "stunts" like getting a local circus to paint one of the elephants white and walk it on Main Street for a Chamber of Commerce "White Elephant Sale Day."

"There must be a better way to make a living than this," he thought to himself. I taught him the art of cosmic attunement. He practiced this daily for a few weeks.

Then things started to happen. He was called in by the local school system. They needed the education story told to the local community to create support for the program when budget voting time came around. He was retained on an annual basis. Another board of education heard about him, then another. The mayor of his town retained him to help with the town image. Within a year, he had a half dozen of these high-paying governmental clients, valid sources of news, and higher levels of uses for his public relations talents.

No more stunts and circuses. And a lot more money.

What is cosmic attunement? It is a special kind of Alpha Picturing. In order to explain it, let me remind you of the metaphysical actions that you already know about:

- You can use your consciousness to clear your own personality.
- You can use it to leave your body and go through walls.
- You can use it to travel great distances.
- You can use it to affect other people.

- You can use it for thought world creations that have real effects in the material world (such as the room you just made for luck).

Now let me clue you in as to other uses you will be making of your consciousness.

- You will use it to move forward and backward in time.
- You will use it to enter the consciousness of another person.
- You will use it to overcome the apparent separateness between you and the rest of the world.

It is this latter use of consciousness—uniting with the universe—that is the secret of cosmic attunement. It is the one metaphysical act that can create the greatest miracles in your life.

Are you ready to make yourself part of something bigger than you? That's a tall order. We are living our lives as if we are our bodies. It is so tall, weighs so many pounds. It hurts, it hinders, it hungers, it pleasures.

Metaphysicians have known for ages that we are not our bodies. Our bodies are just vehicles for who we really are. Just like a car needs gas, has to be washed, provided with new shoes, occasionally repaired, and eventually winds up in the junk heap, so it is with our bodies.

But not so with our consciousness. Consciousness is energy, not matter. Energy is never destroyed. It just changes form. We are not our bodies. Whoever we really are is certainly more attached to the energy of consciousness than to the body.

If you can accept yourself as your consciousness . . .If you can accept the existence of a larger consciousness of which you are part, that is, the consciousness that is behind the order, intelligence, and purpose apparent in the universe, then you are ready to permit your consciousness to "shake hands" with this cosmic Consciousness.

It is the greatest step anybody can ever take in his life. It opens you up to the greatest good luck, the most astounding "miracles," a veritable storehouse of love, power, and good fortune. It is as if the cosmic Consciousness has been waiting for this moment. "I thought you would never recognize me."

You will find that this is the most pleasant feeling you ever experienced in a relaxed way. It is as if something inside you is also jubilant at the union or reunion. Like two old friends getting together after many years—or a long separated father and son, mother and daughter.

What do you get? You get a lot. If I were to list all the possible things that you become eligible to receive, it would only confuse you. Let me simplify it by saying: *You get whatever you need to accomplish your goals in life.*

That sounds like a big order. It is. But it is yours to have.

An actor lands a leading role.

A struggling accountant is made vice president of a large firm.

A widow is made social hostess at a large hotel.

An unemployed, young intellectual simultaneously receives two part-time posts, assisting professors of religion and philosophy at the local university.

Mrs. I.E. performed this metaphysical project when her life seemed at a dead end. Her husband drank heavily. He had no ambition. Their house seemed more a prison than a home. Within a few months, her husband began to drink less and less frequently. They sold the house and bought a farm. They both found excitement and challenge in growing vegetables, and taking care of their thriving orchards. She studied metaphysics intensely and then began to teach it, with her husband one of her ardent students.

So if you have prepared yourself by doing the previous metaphysical projects, here, for you, is the big one:

Metaphysical Action Plan for Harnessing Cosmic Power in Your Life

1. Relax very deeply, taking a few extra minutes to sink into a blissful state of total tranquility.

2. Visualize yourself surrounded by a beautiful blue sky. The blue was never so intense, never so magnificent. It attracts you almost like a member of the opposite sex.

3. You reach upward with your mind, your consciousness seeking to embrace the blue sky, to enfold it in love.

4. As your consciousness ascends upward to embrace the blue, it gradually becomes brilliant white. This brilliance is even more attractive to you but in a different way. It is like the brilliance of a great person you yearn to be near. You continue your ascendance to enfold this greatness.

5. A great feeling of love comes over you. The brilliant whiteness seems to dissolve in it. You sit immersed in it for several minutes.

6. You end your session at the count of five.

The Miraculous Link
Between You and the Universe

Metaphysical miracles are brought about by small people as well as big people, by poor people as well as rich people, by man or woman, young or old.

All have consciousness. And that consciousness is part of universal consciousness. But universal consciousness is a free consciousness. It splits off, separates, manifests itself in a plant, a bird, or you.

The plant "knows" things that are going on at great distances away. In their book, *The Secret Life of Plants*,[2] Peter Tompkins and Christopher Bird report on scientific research that indicates plants grow to please people, that plants move, albeit slowly, and can even open doors, that plants have ESP, and that plants communicate with the outer world, and can be used to predict hurricanes, tornadoes, and volcanic eruptions.

So the plant "knows" it is part of a universal consciousness.

The birds fly great distances without erring as much as a radar equipped plane. They, too, are aware of natural changes even before they occur. They tune in to the universal consciousness of which they "know" they are part.

Only men feel separate. And so man lives with his consciousness separated from the universal consciousness. Whenever a man decides to unite his consciousness with universal consciousness, he can, merely by agreeing to do it. Then miracles begin to happen. He makes the right decisions automatically. He wants the things he really needs. He moves his life in the direction that fits his unique capabilites. And he flourishes accordingly.

He or she. You are now that man, or that woman. You have the whole cosmos working with you. You are connected to a power source greater than the atom. Improve that connection by repeating the previous metaphysical action plan once a day.

Welcome.

[2]Peter Tompkins and Christopher Bird, *The Secret Life of Plants*, (New York, N.Y.: Harper and Row, 1973).

5

How Miracle Metaphysics Draws the Love Mate of Your Choice to Your Side

Love is the greatest power in the universe. It can drive men and women to commit the most heinous crimes. Or it can lift them to the highest peaks of ecstasy.

To be without a lover is to be empty. To be without the person you long for is to be driven to desperation.

You need no longer suffer from loneliness of unrequited love. Those days are past. You now have the power to draw to your side the love mate of your choice. This chapter tells you how to use that power right now.

How Stephen R. Used a Piece of Her Clothing to Make Her Travel One Thousand Miles to Be with Him

Stephen R. and Lucille were to be married. But she met somebody else who, she said, needed her more. She flew to Chicago with this other man, leaving Stephen crushed in spirit and wallowing in despair. But not for long. He used the power of metaphysics this way.

Lucille had left her equestrian gear with him—riding habit and boots. He used these as a psychic "lever" by holding them and Alpha Picturing that they really were not just clothing but part of Lucille herself. If he touched them, she would feel his love.

Now he was ready to exert his metaphysical power. He took the clothes in his car when he went to work. He placed them in his bed when he went to sleep. He talked to them occasionally, caressed them, and, once a day, reinforced his Alpha Picturing of this clothing as part of Lucille herself.

In a few months, Lucille called from Chicago. Would he take her back? Stephen played it cool, just told her he would meet her at the airport.

Two weeks later, they were married.

The knowledge we are acquiring about the power of the consciousness is beginning to throw some light on why ancient love potions and magical incantations work.

How to Put Charms and Incantations to Work for You

One of the rites of ancient Tahiti prior to an armed conflict between clans was the close examination of the entrails of a pig. They did not just cut open a pig and file by and look at the innards. They spent all day at it.

I'm sure you can understand what was going on. These Tahitian warriors were associating the enemy with the entrails. They were doing so in both a relaxed way—Alpha Picturing—and in an emotionally charged way—chanting and dancing. They needed to charge themselves up with metaphysical power and also weaken the enemy by tying him to death.

If you do not know about the energy of consciousness, you look at this ancient Tahitian ritual as superstition. However, now you see its validity. You see the connection between Stephen's Alpha Picturing of his loved one with her clothing and the Tahitian spearman's trance-like viewing of the dead pig. In both cases the energy of consciousness was being put to work in a very realistic way.

Many charms and incantations go even further than the power of your consciousness when you use them. Suppose you were walking along the sidewalk and somebody called you by name. You looked but did not recognize the person. Calling you by name again, he asked, "Can you help me put this package in my car?" Certainly you would walk over to help. You would be drawn to do so.

Now you might be drawn out of curiosity, out of vanity, out of compassion. It does not really matter. What matters is that you are drawn.

Ancient charms and incantations are like calling someone's name. I did not say "somebody," I said someone. That is because the ancient sounds and symbols are like calling the names of consciousnesses no longer in the body.

The second law of thermodynamics says that energy is never destroyed. It merely changes in form. The energy of your consciousness can never die. Your body may no longer be an adequate home or vehicle for your consciousness, but your energy of consciousness does not "die."

It is the combined energies of certain consciousnesses that are "called" when you use an old incantation or charm. They come to your aid. It does not matter if you need help in lifting a package into your car or attracting a loved one to your side. . .

You call these energies to your support when you recite something that is quite familiar to them or perform a ritual used thousands of times in the past and to which they respond. It is like calling their name.

People often inadvertently call for such support—sometimes when it would be better not to have it. For instance, you are in a violent fight with somebody. Tempers have flared to the boiling point. You are in a rage. He hits you. You reach for a vase and raise it over your head . . . .

At that very moment, all the energies on the wavelength—a wavelength of violence and destruction—come to your assistance. Wham!

Later, you say, "I don't know what came over me."

Prof. William Tenhaeff, hailed as the "father of parapsychology," believes people have the ability to tune into a vast universal mind shared by all. When we die, he says, our mind goes back into this pool of universal mind.

This concept seems to be growing in acceptance by both the scientific and spiritual world. It certainly helps to explain the awesome metaphysical power that we can tap if we know how.

In this universal mind are romantic energies that come to your help if you trigger your own mind properly. Using a possession, a strand of hair, or a piece of clothing of a loved one can be that trigger. Here is how to proceed to attract a loved one who has left you, back to your arms.

Metaphysical
Action
Plan for
Attracting
Back a
Loved One

1. Hold object of loved one in your hand and go to your alpha level.
2. Alpha Picture your loved one. Place object next to your heart. See your loved one turn to you, smiling and reaching out to you.
3. Repeat several times, knowing that whenever you touch the object to the heart area, the loved one "feels" this and responds.
4. End session.

Keep the object around where you can pick it up frequently and touch it to your heart. You will not have long to wait before your loved one returns.

The Seal of Solomon
Magnifies Your Power of Attraction

The power of love is greater than the power of destruction. It is even easier to get help from consciousnesses in the name of love than it is in the name of violence.

So you can expect an even easier time of it to get support for your effort to attract a loved one than to smash an enemy.

The Seal of Solomon is an example. Let me tell you about it. And then I'll tell you how easy it is to use it.

The Hebrew Kabbala, or Science of the Prophets, is a book containing the ancient mysteries known only to Jewish rabbis of old. It was written in such a way that even if the book came into undeserving hands the secrets would not be evident. In other words, it was written quite esoterically. The average man sees it only as a collection of riddles.

However, the secrets of the Kabbala are now being revealed. Mankind is ready to use the power of metaphysics. Occult matters are being de-occulted. "Mysterious power" and "secret science" are words often applied to the Kabbala. But gradually, the "secrets" are being decoded and the "mysteries" are being understood.

To give you an idea how difficult it is to unravel these mysteries, take the hint given in the Bible that "In the beginning was the Word." Charles W. Littlefield, M.D., researched this secret at the turn of this

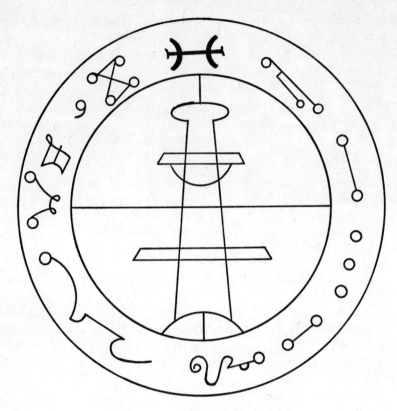

Plate I

century. Using mineral salts, he was able to create crystal forms by
imaging them. Watching through a microscope, he saw matter become
the obedient servant of his mind with "exactness that must be due to
some marvelous law we cannot understand."

"The Word," it appears, can be a spoken word or an image. Either
can be creative. We cannot understand why, but the words we speak
and the images we hold in our mind are creative forces that tend to
"produce" in kind.

"I can't go out with you tonight," a young man told a girl he was
trying to break off with. "My grandmother died." Three days later, his
fib came true.

Transcendental Meditation is the use of mantras, or holy words,
repeated again and again to elevate the consciousness. They work
whether you know what the words mean or not.

Mental images were often reproduced in the form of pictorial signs and symbols by the ancients. These diagrams still retain the power originally invested in them by the mental imaging that created them.

Use these diagrams today and you perform creative acts which defy explanation.

Such a diagram (Plate I) is Solomon's Seal. It has the power to bring two people together. This power goes back thousands of years, which seems like the dim, dim past to us but in reality is but a second in the history of creation.

Are you yearning to be with a certain person? Would you like to have that person drawn to your side as if by some unseen power?

Solomon's Seal will help to do it. But there is a price to pay.

The price is you must be willing to permit that person to leave if that is his or her will. The Seal will not control. It can only send an irresistible attractive force to bring you together.

In other words, it can bring you together, but it cannot keep you together. Sometimes it is quite painful to have to separate. It may not be necessary, but if it is, you must be willing to pay that price.

Here is how to use Solomon's Seal to attract somebody to your side:

Metaphysical Action Plan for Attracting a Person to Your Side with Solomon's Seal

1. Trace the Seal onto a piece of white paper.
2. Obtain a photo of the person or make a sketch which represents that person to you.
3. Go to your alpha level. Feel great respect for the power of the Seal.
4. While at your alpha level, place the Seal together with the picture, face to face, feeling part of the person in the sketch of picture.
5. End your alpha session.
6. Keep the Seal and Picture with you wherever you go, still face to face, and under your pillow at night, until the two of you meet.

Before you actually perform this powerful metaphysical act, let me give you some further help.

When tracing the seal, if emotional needs are the motive for wanting to be with the person—the most common, of course, being love or physical attraction—use a red crayon or felt pen. If you can use a luminescent red as is frequently available in art supply stores, it will add "light" (and greater power) to the procedure.

If the motive is mental or intellectual, having to do with the person's fine intelligence, use yellow as your tracing color. If money or health is involved, use green. If there is a spiritual motive, use blue.

As you trace, feel that your own consciousness is at work. The less automatic you perform the tracing, the better. Be aware of the sanctity of the Seal you are creating. Fill your consciousness, adding energy to the already powerful design.

When you obtain a photo or make a sketch of the person, look at it as not merely the photo or sketch but the real thing. See it as a living "shadow" of the person you want to attract.

The moment of placing the two together, face to face, should be a "high" moment for you, even though you are thoroughly relaxed. Feel the greatness of Solomon. Feel the sacred nature of the ancient Seal. Feel the importance of the moment. Feel the contact between Seal and photo as the moment of your actual coming together.

Be aware of the Seal and picture or sketch as you carry it with you. This occasional remembering of its presence should *never* be in the spirit of questioning—"Will it happen?" or "When will it happen?" Always remember its presence in the spirit of happy expectation—a pleasant reunion to the both of you.

"It works!" How many times I have heard that when the Seal of Solomon is used to attract a member of the opposite sex!

"She called me the next day. She came over that night. But she hasn't been back since. It's over a week now, what do I do?"

"Forget her."

In this case, the Seal of Solomon did its work: to bring two people together. It does not promise to enslave.

One woman psychologist gave up her practice to travel with a metaphysical lecturer who had wanted her badly (or goodly) enough to use the Seal. She traveled with him wherever he went, but the relationship lasted only three months.

You can use the Seal of Solomon to attract to you whomever you wish. From then on it becomes a different kind of a problem, requiring different magic. The Seal's job is to bring man and woman together.

And it works!

The Role the Swastika
Can Play in Your Love Life

The culmination of love is depicted in many they-lived-happily-ever-after legends. The true culmination of love from the universal view is the bearing of a child. A child gives living power to the love relationship. Cultures throughout the world use metaphysical energy to insure fertility.

Rods, ploughs, staffs, and sceptres appear repeatedly in ancient art. They are symbols of the phallic power and of the act of insemination.

The cross antedates Christianity and is said to have originally been Stone Age man's way of fixing the four cardinal directions. Later it came to symbolize creative phallic power and sexual fulfillment.

The armed cross, known as the swastika, evolved from the cross. It came to symbolize the moving seasons. It has been found all the way from the American Indians to Congo natives. A swastika rotating counterclockwise is life-destroying and unlucky. But a swastika turning clockwise is life supporting and used as a fertility-granting symbol.

Hitler was advised by his metaphysicians to use the clockwise swastika in the flag of the Nazi Third Reich. How he created a powerful political organization under this flag is history. But when destruction was perpetrated under this flag, the Third Reich itself was destroyed.

You can use the creative swastika, the one turning clockwise (see Plate II), to add "life" to your romance. However, if you do, be ready for it to power *his* potency and *her* fertility. Here is how to proceed:

Metaphysical Action Plan to Add Life to Your Romance with the Swastika	1. Mount the clockwise swastika between photos of each of you. 2. Place it on the door of the bedroom. Hang something over it if you wish to use this in secret. 3. Look at it three times a day. 4. Alpha Picture it before you retire.

Plate II

How to Whisper Magic Words
That Act as Love Commands

The use of talismans like a piece of clothing, seals like that of Solomon, and symbols like the clockwise swastika are powerful reinforcement to your own conscious energy. But you have all the metaphysical power you need built into you to make your love irrestible.

In the beginning was the word. Your word is still an omnipotent force, able to cut through obstacles and impediments and manifest a life as you see it.

The power of your word can:

● Bring flowers from your boyfriend even though it is not your birthday.

● Have her phone you for a date even if you have not seen her for a year.

● Cause a frigid person to suddenly become passionately affectionate.

● Release yosr sexual partner from inhibitions or hangups.

● Build up peaks of ecstasy to heights never before reached.

Here is the secret: The creative pozer of your word is unleashed when it is *whispered* at the *alpha* level. So here is what you do.

Metaphysical Action Plan for Using Words of Love That Act as Commands

1. Relax and visualize your loved one.

2. Move your lips to the left ear (on your right if the image is facing you).

3. Whisper words or love audibly, feeling the bliss that you would feel if your heads were actually that close together.

4. End your relaxation on a note of expectancy.

Expect a response from your loved one. He or she will not know just why they are taking a loving step toward you. But take it, they will.

How Roland L. Used Whispered Commands That Triggered Her to Respond Passionately to Him

Roland L. had been living with a beautiful Oriental girl, a fellow student at the University. "It was an exciting relationship at the outset," he related. "But now, six months later, we just seem to go through the motions. She doesn't get excited, so I don't respond the way I used to. What can I do?"

I taught Roland Alpha Picturing. This he used to visualize his girl friend in his arms, reacting passionately to his touch, to his embrace, and to his kisses as he whispered over and over again in her left ear, "I love you."

The results were instantaneous and as far as I know this second "honeymoon" may still be on.

The Secret That Can Make the Opposite Sex Swarm Around You Like a Hungry Mob

You can use metaphysical power on yourself to enhance your attraction to the opposite sex. In this case, it is the insertion of a secret ingredient into your personality. You program this ingredient into your subconscious and in return, it programs you for subtle behavior.

This subtle behavior in a woman attracts men like flies. In a man, it pulls the women to him as if by some irresistible force.

Before I tell you what that ingredient is let me just say that when you hear it, the word may not have the same meaning to you as it has for the metaphysician. You may say, "Oh, I tried that," or "Yes, that's fine, but . . ." or "I won't buy that." Hear me through. Then try it. You may find that it doesn't "taste" bad after all and can be the very "love potion" you need.

The secret is super self-confidence.

You do not have to have it. All you have to do is express it. Even if you have it, you can express it more unmistakably and heighten your sexual attraction immensely.

Confidence speaks sexual reams. The confident male inspires confidence in the female and vice versa. A ten minute Alpha Picturing session with yourself can automatically get you to radiate a man of the world or woman of the world charisma even if deep inside you know you're as green as an unripe apple.

How Betty L. Changed His Hostility into Endearment in Hours

Betty L. was living with a psychologist in the Washington, D.C., area. She had hopes of marriage, but they had been together a year now and their communication seemed to be breaking down. He "put down"

everything she said. She was always wrong. And he was always quick
to criticize her. Naturally, the relationship was deteriorating.

I met them at a convention of psychologists. At the first opportunity, when her psychologist friend was leading a seminar, she sought
my advice.

"I just don't know what to do about us," she sobbed through her
tears, which had begun to flow with her first words. "Everything I say
irritates him."

After listening for a few minutes and permitting her to release her
anxiety by venting it, I asked her, "Do you know the greatest sexual
weapon that woman has?"

"No," she said, dabbing at her eyes.

"It is silence."

"Silence? But what brought us together was our initial interest in
people and their psychological responses."

"But it is not keeping you together, is it?"

"No."

"Try silence. Try it tonight."

She agreed. What I did not tell her was that silence expressed a
great metaphysical power—super self-confidence.

That evening I spotted the two dining at the hotel restaurant across
from me. The psychologist was doing the talking. Her lips moved only
to eat. When they got up to leave, I saw the psychologist go to her side
of the table, take her face in his hands and kiss her on the lips. The next
morning, when she passed me in the convention hall, she gave me a
big wink.

Silence is not the only way that super self-confidence is expressed. I don't want you to set your mind on using silence. It may
be correct for you but it also may not be.

What you need to do is to "zap" yourself with the power of super
self-confidence and let yourself express it in whatever natural ways that
your subconscious mind, and body, select. Here are some ways that
super self-confidence can be unconsciously expressed:

- A girl leans nonchalantly on her elbow, swinging her crossed leg.
- A man hooks his thumbs under his belt, fingers pointing down.
- A girl leans closely toward a man she has just met, her shoulder
  touching his.
- A man puffs seriously on his cigarette, ignoring everybody around
  him.

The girl's name might be Miss Wallflower. The man's name might be Mr. Milquetoast. Neither programmed themselves to behave that way. Both programmed themselves metaphysically with Alpha Picturing to express super self-confidence.

It won't be long before both have enjoyed such exciting sexual conquests that their super self-confidence will perpetuate and strengthen itself.

Turn Up Your Sexual Attraction with These Powerful Commands

Are you ready for the opposite sex to feel your presence like never before? Then proceed with this programming as follows:

Metaphysical Action Plan for Acquiring Intensified Sexual Attraction	1. Relax. 2. Say out loud in a commanding voice: "My confidence as a (male) (female) is now increasing. I feel more and more confident with the opposite sex. I am more and more attractive to the opposite sex." 3. Visualize yourself standing erect and radiating youthful attraction, surrounded by admiring members of the opposite sex. 4. End your relaxation.

Perform this session several times a day for a few days and you will see changes in yourself . . .changes that will put the opposite sex in the palm of your hand.

How to Use the Hypnotic Eye on Members of the Opposite Sex

If you were to recall your favorite movie star, you would probably remember the eyes—how large and expressive they were. In all cultures of the world, large eyes are considered a strong asset.

Psychologists have recently discovered that the pupil of the eye expands when a person sees something he likes. Also, there is a contraction of the pupil when a person sees something he does not like. In fact, some psychologists have used this as a diagnostic test. They show a male client a picture of a nude male. Normally, his pupils should contract or show no effect. If they dilate, he could have homosexual tendencies.

You have been noticing this unconsciously for years. You see people's eyes "light up" and you know they are glad to see you; whereas, with a person who is angry, the eyes become narrow slits.

Other people respond to the way you use your eyes. Your eyes can become a hypnotic force without the use of hypnotism.

It is easy to do. Here is all there is to it:

Metaphysical Action Plan to Use the Hypnotic Eye

1. When you wish to influence a member of the opposite sex, hold eye contact longer than usual.

2. Open the aperture of your eyelids slightly. Do not stare but move your eyes closer to staring.

3. After a few minutes of steps 1 and 2, express your wish in your usual way. It will very likely be agreed to.

A steady gaze speaks confidence and maturity. You are looked up to as a fascinating person. You win admiration and respect.

A wider aperture in your eyelids creates the impression of dilated pupils. *Result:* Extreme interest in you, as reciprocation, is felt in a positive way by a member of the opposite sex.

You have demonstrated the power of the hypnotic eye. In a future chapter, you will learn to use the pendulum, among other things, as a metaphysical tool to acquire the innermost secrets of people. These you can use to expand your control over him or her, and to test whether this is the right person for you.

Meanwhile, maybe what were social and sexual fiascos now become for you and yours, crescendo after crescendo of ecstasy.

6

How Miracle Metaphysics Attracts Wealth to You Faster Than You Can Spend It

Money is the symbol of abundance. The flow of money into and out of men's lives is probably, next to love, man's greatest concern.

This concern for money seems to have a strange effect: The rich get richer and the poor get poorer. This has been recognized even as far back as the writing of the Bible.

You can understand this apparent unfairness now that you have reached this chapter better than you probably could have understood it before you opened this book. You can see how a poor man who visualizes his lack and worries about his tomorrow, perpetuates that lack. While the rich man who mentally counts his wealth and anticipates its growth, perpetuates his abundance.

Change your habitual thinking from thoughts of limited money to thoughts of unlimited wealth and you change your life. However, this is not easily done. How can you think of wealth when you have more bills to pay than you have cash in the bank? How can you think of wealth when a note is due or the car is on its last legs?

Metaphysics enables you to turn the tide. This chapter contains the "white magic" of creating all the wealth you need.

How Pamela B. Used a Special One Dollar Bill to Start a Flow of Thousands of Dollars That Is Still Continuing

Mrs. Pamela B. was starting a metaphysical book store in Canada. She wrote me asking for any psychic support I could send her.

When I read the letter, I took a dollar bill out of my pocket and held it for a moment in my hand. I "saw" this dollar bill moving out into circulation creating an ever expanding stream of returning dollar bills.

"Good luck," I wrote her. "This dollar is not to be framed. Spend it for something right away and then watch what happens."

Two months later we met at a metaphysical conference. Her face lit up like a beacon when she spotted me. "That dollar bill," she reported, "has not stopped flowing yet. It's a miracle."

She told me how she gave it to a high school student for helping her place books on the shelves. The student told others about the "far out books" in her store. Clubs formed. Teachers called her in to describe her store to their classes. Students are now her best customers and bringing in their parents, too.

That dollar is still flooding her with more thousands of dollars today.

Later in this chapter I will tell you how to energize money to create your own flood of cash. But first you have some mental work to do.

This is a world of abundance. Nature casts her seeds around as if they were going out of style. It takes one sperm to fertilize an egg. But is nature a piker? Have yourself a million.

Abundance seems to flow naturally through some people, but not through others. If you are in this latter group, I have some shocking news for you: A torrent of wealth has been ready to flow through your hands, but . . .you have been blocking it.

Here is how to get out of your own way and permit yourself to have all the money you need.

A Powerful Mantra That Materializes Money

Let's get inside Henry's head and listen to his thoughts. Henry is in between jobs.

"Five dollars has to last me until tomorrow . . . .What if the unemployment check is late? . . .I'll take her to the pizza parlor tonight . . . .Hope the gas holds out . . . I'll stay out until after the landlady goes to bed . . . .Hard to find a job . . . ."

Now let's get inside Fred's head and listen to his thoughts. Fred is in between his first and second million.

"Have to switch banks and get that higher interest rate. . . .Ought

to start my own bank . . . .I'll give her a car for her birthday . . . .Never been to Bali, think I'll go . . . .Probably can open up
some new markets in the Orient . . . ."

The pictures in Henry's head are free. True or false? False. Those
pictures are costing Henry a fortune. It is the same kind of fortune that
Fred is enjoying.

Well, you say, Henry and Fred are both picturing what they already have. True. But now for the good news: The picture comes first.

The choice of pictures is yours. You can have all the pictures of
abundance you can imagine. The more you picture, the more abundant
your life becomes.

Here's the hitch. It is next to impossible to think realistically of
riches when your stomach is empty. And how can you visualize
thousands in the bank when you just received a notice you're over-
drawn?

What is needed first is a sort of mental aspirin—something to ease
the pain of poverty so you can better visualize wealth.

Here is just what the doctor ordered—the "meta" physician, that
is. Do it now.

Metaphysical Action Plan to Change from A Consciousness Of Poverty to One of Wealth Using a Mantra of Abundance

1. Memorize these words: "Nature expresses abundance through me. I open myself to the flow of opportunity and wealth. OM. OM. OM." Pronounced as in "home."

2. Relax and picture yourself as wealthy. Let pictures of office, home, and family flow through your mind, reflecting dreams come true.

3. End by repeating the words you memorized in (1) three times.

This is an affirmation reinforced by a mantra. The affirmation is
the part you memorized; the mantra the final word, "OM."

Let me explain OM. It is a sanctified sound. Sacred not because
it is some particular culture's deity or blessing, but because it is the
sound of nature herself! If all the spheres in the universe made a sound,
if all the molecules vibrating in matter could be heard, if all the electrons rotating in atoms were audible, the sound would be like "singing" OM in a monotone.

Keep your lips open as you sound it. Feel how you vibrate to this
sound. Everything resonates to this universal sound.

Test this out. Hold your hands out in front of you, palms down. Now sing "OM" in a low monotone. Can you "hear" the sound with the skin of your palms? Your palms tingle as it vibrates to the mantra.

The effect of OM on you is to open you to the universe. You become more aligned with universal flows of all kinds—the flow of order, growth, intelligence, harmony, and abundance.

The science of psychotronics, study of consciousness, is confirming the validity of ancient metaphysical prosperity practices. Where consciousness aligns itself with the universe, you automatically remove those private little dams you have built. And the natural flow of wealth enters your life.

The Wheel of Fortune and How to Make It Spin a Fortune for You

A state of consciousness is induced by the input of our senses. Sights and sounds of limited money are the main sensory input, but there are also the touch, taste and smell of limited money: the touch of worn-out carpeting, the taste of frankfurters and beans, the smell of musty wood.

Sight is by far the most important input. It is estimated that some 80% of our total environmental input is optical. That is why picturing is so important.

In the previous action plan we used sight and sound. We need to do more having to do with sight. The ancients knew this. So they created the Wheel of Fortune. (See Plate III.)

Found in many cultures, the wheel of fortune is symbolically the wheel of life. Although you may find one in some art reference book, it is best to draw your own, knowing that you are creating "avenues" for the flow of wealth with each spoke you draw.

There is a sign for OM. You are the hub of the wheel, the center of your universe. You can write the word "me." But the OM sign is a more powerful symbol to put at the center of your wheel of fortune. Label the spokes of the wheel with the qualities you aim for in your life, such as courage, honesty, generosity, compassion, strength, and so on.

Around the line you draw for the rim of the wheel, write your own affirmation of abundance. Here are some examples:

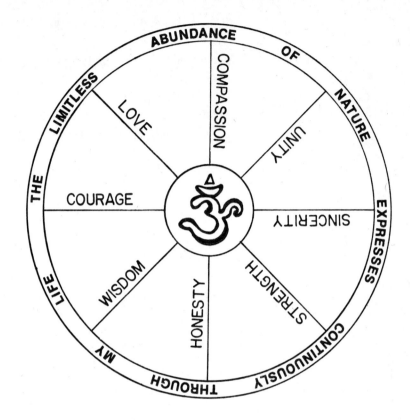

Plate III

Spiritual affirmation. "The God power within me provides abundantly for all of my needs."

Scientific affirmation. "Money is energy. The more energy I put out, the more I receive. I grow in wealth."

Philosophical affirmation. "Abundance is Nature's way. I am an expression of Nature. I express abundance."

These should not be my affirmations. They should be your affirmations. Pick the kind you are most comfortable with. The spiritual kind is the most powerful.

Place the finished drawing of your wheel of fortune in some prominent place in your house so you see it frequently, even if only in a passing way. But before you do so, perform this metaphysical activation of it:

Metaphysical Action Plan for Energizing a Wheel of Fortune to Release a Continuous Flood of Wealth

1. Hold the sheet of paper with the wheel of fortune on it in your hand as you relax.

2. Place the wheel of fortune about six inches from your eyes while at the alpha level.

3. See the spokes as extending outward into every aspect of your life, reaping a crop of abundance and wealth that surges through you as you go forth.

4. End your session and post the wheel of fortune.

Your wheel of fortune is now a Wheel of Fortune.

You need not be conscious of it for it to work. If it is on the refrigerator door, every time you pass the refrigerator, you reinforce its power in you.

I have never heard of a case where the wheel of fortune did not work financial good in the life of its creator. Its effects may not be as dramatic as coming into a bundle of cash or inheriting an oil well. But everything becomes generally better for you as needs are met and financial limitations melt away.

How Steve B. Used Affirmation and Mantra to Crawl Out from Under a Pile of Bills into a Life of Ease

Steve B. had been married for ten years when his business went bankrupt leaving him with nothing but bills. The bank was threatening to foreclose on his home. The phone was cut off. The electric company was breathing down his neck. Bill collectors had stopped threatening and were serving summons. To get cash for food, Steve was kiting checks at the banks, an illegal procedure that was bound to catch up with him soon.

Steve had been interested in metaphysics, but now this passing interest became his last resort. He applied the affirmation of wealth in his life several times a day and sang the OM mantra. He also visualized himself free of his problems. Within three months he had renegotiated his mortgage with another bank, leaving him excess funds to pay all his bills. He had started a new business which was earning more than enough for his family, and he started to accumulate savings.

If you have used the OM mantra and created a wheel of fortune, you have changed the polarity of your consciousness. You are now able to perform amazing metaphysical money feats.

How to Energize a Dollar Bill
to Multiply Manyfold Again and Again

At the beginning of this chapter I told you the story of how I energized a dollar bill for Pamela B. and how it brought her a continuous flood of dollars. You are now able to create this same exciting phenomena—for yourself or for others.

I have seen this work for many people:

- A young man got an unexpected tax refund of $150 that same week.
- A woman found a $20 bill that same day.
- A writer got a $5,000 assignment in three weeks.
- A real estate woman, with no sale for months, made a $3,000 commission within three days.

How Mrs. Norma E. Made a $3,000
Commission with a Charged $1 Bill

Mrs. Norma E. was a moderately successful real estate agent. But sales had been few and far between for nearly a year. A seller's market had turned to a buyer's market and a large influx of new real estate agents were competing for the thinner market.

With three youngsters to feed and both a home and office to maintain, Mrs. E. was feeling very low when she came to me for metaphysical assistance. I had her put a dollar bill in front of her, and then had her relax and picture sunlight entering her body and then beaming out to the money from her solar plexus. She saw the money charged with energy so that when she spent it, it would return manyfold. She was the dollar triggering a deluge of dollars in her direction. Then she spent the dollar.

Three days after this exercise she received a call from a couple she showed a house to ten weeks before but who had decided to buy elsewhere.

"We're back," he said. "If that house is still available, we"ll take it at the asking price." The sale meant a much needed $3,000 commission to Mrs. E. and a financial turn of events in her career.

Coincidence? Maybe. But metaphysicians certainly attract more than their share of happy "coincidences."

You have prepared your consciousness to accept unlimited abundance. You will now learn how to prepare a "triggering device" that can set off an explosion of wealth. That device is a dollar bill. It can also be a five, ten, or twenty. Wait until you have successes with these denominations before you use larger bills as your triggering device:

Here is how to proceed:

Metaphysical
Action
Plan to
Charge
Up a
Dollar
Bill as a
Triggering
Device to
Set Off an
Explosion of
Money

1. Relax with the bill in your hand.

2. Visualize the sun above your head, beating down on you with brilliance and warmth.

3. See that sunlight entering your solar plexus (just above your navel.) Permit it to enter for a few minutes.

4. Now hold the dollar bill to your solar plexus. See it being charged by the sun's energy that you have stored.

5. When it appears to get hot in your hand, visualize yourself spending the bill and its energy touching off a flow of bills in your direction. See it continuing to do this wherever it goes.

6. End the session and spend the bill as quickly as possible.

How to Multiply the Deluge of Money by Combining Your Power With Others

Where consciousness goes, energy goes. I keep repeating this because it is *the* new concept of this age. The ancients knew it. But then mankind seemed to forget it. The energy of consciousness is now being rediscovered and harnessed to do work.

You energized a dollar bill (or higher denomination) to do work utilizing the energy of your consciousness. You used your consciousness as a battery.

Two batteries provide more energy than one. Three, of course, more than two.

You can build up the energy flow into a bill by working with your friends or members of your family. They must not oppose the action out of disbelief. This would short-circuit the energy. They must believe as you believe, do as you do:

Metaphysical Action Plan to Build Up Conscious Energy by Joining with Others

1. Review procedure as all sit in a circle.
2. Place one bill in center of circle (repeat process later if more than one bill is to be energized).
3. Clasp hands, left palms up, right palms down.
4. Proceed as in previous Action Plan.

Every philosopher and metaphysician knows that the universe does not give you something for nothing. But they also know that you have a huge credit built up with the universe because if you are like most people, you have been selling yourself short—accepting less money than you deserve for what you do, getting no money for many services you render, and thinking less of yourself and your worth than your true value.

So, the OM mantra, the wheel of fortune, and the metaphysical dollar bill are ways of opening your previously locked doors of consciousness and permitting the universe to pay its debt to you. This debt may run into the thousands of dollars or even hundreds of thousands of dollars. But then there comes a time when you must keep the flow going by building up your credit with the universe.

Before I set forth the procedure for building up this credit, let me review what you must do to keep your consciousness open to the money deluge.

- Repeat the OM mantra periodically.
- Keep a wheel of fortune in sight.
- Charge up a bill occasionally and send it out.
- Keep a bill of large proportions hidden on your person ($20, $50—as in your clothing or purse or wallet compartment).
- Repeat the affirmation on the rim of your wheel of fortune several times a day.

How to Keep Money Flowing to You from Many Directions

Do you have a valuable gift or talent? Have you ever helped others to develop a similar talent? When writers freely help others to write, musicians help others to play, accountants give pointers to newcomers to their profession, good things happen to these good Samaritans. Since the person helped does not pay them, the universe must pay them,

When the universe pays you, it pays you much better than people pay you. Try it in the next few days. Do something of value for which you get no payment. Here are some possibilities:

- Help someone to learn English.
- Volunteer your time at a hospital.
- Join a fraternal or service organization.
- Write a letter to your editor or your congressman in favor of some reform.
- Read for the blind.
- Spend time at an orphanage.
- Be a companion to some lonely senior citizen.
- Help your neighbor with that planting or construction project.
- Stay overtime voluntarily to help the firm get a particular job done.

How is helping your neighbor, a friend, or your boss a metaphysical act? Try it and see.

First, you will receive gifts from people. Maybe they are not even the people you did something for. Accept these gifts graciously, knowing that these people are just playing a role of the universe. They have been moved to make you the recipient of their apple pie, the coconut from Jamaica, or the dress or suit they changed their mind about.

Second, good things will happen to you. Marcus Bach calls it serendipity. What is serendipity?

You may meet a person who has exactly the answer you need to move ahead on some project. Somebody you have forgotten about may return money you loaned him years ago. A magazine may accept a poem you sent them and enclose a check. The boss may invite you to dinner. These are all examples of serendipity—the universe's way of saying, "Thanks for joining the credit side of the ledger."

The real payment is still to come. The universe pays and pays, way beyond your personal sense of proper remuneration. When you give a book to a hospital library, it may be worth only $1, but the universe weighs more than the retail value of the book. How much is the thought of doing it worth? How much is the motive for bringing pleasure to others worth? How much is that pleasure enjoyed by these others worth?

A metaphysician knows that the wage scale of the universe is beyond belief. The metaphysician gives, gives, and gives, knowing that he is building up treasures beyond description.

You are now a metaphysician. Find out for yourself the real meaning behind the words, "It is better to give than to receive."

Far, far better.

Can You Discover the Ancient Secret of Turning Base Metals into Gold?

In India, a great wise man, Sai Baba, draws thousands to his ashram each day to listen to his teachings, receive his blessings, and observe him produce ash, gems, and gold jewelry, apparently out of the air.

I have personally discussed Sai Baba's abilities with scientists and lay people who have observed him close up. They say it cannot be trickery, but they have no explanation other than that he indeed does what he appears to do: materialize objects.

Sai Baba gives us a clue to the secret behind alchemy—the ability to turn base metals into gold. Perhaps it is not the base metal that is involved but pure consciousness.

Dr. Edgar Mitchell has observed materialization and dematerialization in the laboratory a number of times under fairly well controlled conditions. If the present laws of thermodynamics were all he had to explain this, he comments, San Francisco should have been destroyed by the energy released.

But no energy was measurably released. So something else was involved, which he is now working on.

L.W. deLaurence, whose books on the occult written some fifty years ago are still considered today among the most reliable, claims that the primary material used by alchemists was found within themselves. This then becomes their "philosopher's stone."

Sai Baba has been observed coughing up a stone the size of an egg on numerous occasions. But there has been no claim for these stones in connection with alchemy or materialization of other substances.

If deLaurence is carefully read, one sees a connection between soul essence and a watery mercurial substance which he infers can transmute impure metal into the purest gold and in sizable amounts.

In parts of Africa, it is said that there are "brokers" who enable you to sell your soul for cash. You approach these men and state how much money you need. They in turn tell you how long you may live. You return home and find the cash beneath a pillow or under a bed. Then at the agreed time, one or more years later, you are found dead of unknown causes.

It is unthinkable for a civilized person to sell his soul for cash, but we do it, too, in our own way, as examination of crime records show.

All conjecture, true. But at the rate the occult is being de-occulted these days, the secrets of alchemy are likely to be discovered by somebody soon.

That somebody might be you.

Give the Universe Carte Blanche to Bestow Wealth Upon You

We are in the habit of thinking within limits.

We have undone the financial limitations we formerly placed on ourselves. Abundance can now flow into our life.

However, that habitual way of thinking in terms of limitations can still undercut our metaphysical action plans. The following is an example.

How Mrs. Evelyn V.'s Image of a New Home Backfired

Evelyn V. envied her neighbor across the street who lived in a much bigger house. She visualized herself living in that house. One night she woke up and found her house in flames. Her husband died in the fire. The house was destroyed and all possessions lost. Her neighbor took her in. Thus, in this instance, her vision backfired because of her envy, and her limited vision.

A postal clerk I knew years ago asked me, "You mean to say all I have to do is relax, picture a check for a million dollars and I will get it?"

"Sure," I replied, "If that is really what you want."

A month later he greeted me excitedly with "It worked!" The check writing machine had been set wrong and there was a "1" in the million dollar spot in front of his monthly salary. Of course, the check was useless to him as it could not be legally cashed.

If the mind thinks in limited ways, the Universe replies in kind.

How much better it is to give the Universe a free hand—carte blanche—in channeling wealth to us.

You are better off seeing *a* house instead of *her* house.

You are likely to receive more satisfying results seeing yourself prospering rather than prospering with this person's business or that person's know-how.

How Sam J. Won a $50,000 Lottery

Sam J. needed a grant from the government if he was to continue his research into the powers of the mind. However, instead of the money he received a "don't call us, we'll call you" type of turn down. Now ten years of hard work seemed about to go down the drain.

Sam had become an expert in alpha picturing. He relaxed deeply. He visualized his research not only continuing but expanding. Then he dreamed about a lottery ticket number.

One afternoon he had closed his laboratory and was about to go home when he met a friend.

"Let's cross the border and do shopping before the Mexican stores close," suggested the friend.

Sam agreed. They drove from their Texas town to the Mexican town in just a few minutes. While looking around a store, Sam spotted some lottery tickets. Among them was the number in his dream.

"These are my last few tickets," said the store owner. Sam bought them. A month later he was notified that he had won the equivalent of $50,000. His research was able to continue and he bought some new alpha measuring biofeedback equipment to expand it.

Let the universe decide how it will bestow its blessings on you. You must think wealth. You must think luxury. You must think abundance. You must think travel, possessions, cash in the bank. But let your thoughts be undetailed and unlimited.

Let it happen.

It is yours to enjoy—without limit.

7

Perform Miracle Metaphysical Health Miracles for Youthful Energy and Longer Life

"I have a sinus problem. Nothing seems to help. Can you do anything?"

"My headaches are terrible. Can you help migraine?"

"I can't remember when I've had a good night's sleep. Will I ever get rid of my insomnia?"

These common ailments, as well as a parade of more critically serious diseases, are presented continuously to the metaphysician. Health is man's greatest problem. This is the area where the metaphysical "miracle" is in greatest demand. You can cause healings to take place in yourself and in others.

How Ned B. Helped His Mother off Her Death Bed

Ned B. flew several thousand miles to his stricken mother. The telegram stated she was not expected to survive her combined heart attack and stroke. Ned and other members of the family prayed night and day. The 50-year-old woman managed to hold her own. Doctors said that it was a miracle that she lived but since half her body was paralyzed and her heart badly damaged, they held little hope of her ever walking again.

Ned had to fly back to this job but he enlisted the author's help to use alpha picturing in his mother's behalf. Mental corrections were made in the image of the damaged heart. Nerves were pictured as mending themselves. Within six months, Ned's mother took a trip to visit him and show him living, walking proof of his metaphysical ability.

You are permitted by law to do anything to and for yourself. But . . .

Warning: The law forbids your diagnosing or treating people in matters of health. Do not use the methods in this chapter to tell a person what is wrong with them. Do not use these methods if the person is in your presence. There is no law against absent healing, or spiritual healing.

How to Correct Errors
in Your Internal Health Maker

We are beginning to realize two facts:

1. Every cell and organ in our bodies has a consciousness of its own which is affected by our own mental consciousness.

2. There is an interlacing of energy fields in our body related to consciousness, which are in balance when there is ease of consciousness, out of balance when there is dis-ease of consciousness.

To explain what is meant by the first of these facts let me tell you about the special work of one doctor . . . .

How Dr. Carl Simonton Is Using the Power of His Patients' Consciousnesses to Accelerate Cures

A doctor is teaching mental picturing at alpha levels to his cancer patients with remarkable results. Carl Simonton, M.D., recently reported at a meeting of the Academy of Parapsychology and Medicine just how this has resulted in a marked increase in the rate of recovery of hospitalized cancer patients, when used as a supplement to radiation therapy.

First, Dr. Simonton shows the patient slides of how cancer can and is being cured, thus helping to overcome the feeling of futility that often accompanies this disease. Next, the patient is taught to relax both body and mind. Then, the patient is asked to picture his white blood cells getting rid of cancer cells weakened by radiation.

Each patient is permitted to picture in his own way. One Air Force man, according to Dr. Simonton, pictured his white blood corpuscles as "frogmen"; another patient saw them as "policemen"; a child saw his white blood corpuscles as "cowboys."

They all recovered in rapid time.

Where consciousness goes, energy goes. Your Alpha Picturing can bring health-dealing energy to your body or to others. Your body is like a factory. And you are the boss. That is a pretty hard fact to swallow for most people. We do not like to think we are the cause of our own health problem. It is much more comfortable to blame it on a bug. Then we can go to a doctor for a bug killer or symptom-remover.

Disease-causing viruses and germs are in our body all the time. They multiply and thrive only when we lower our resistance to them.

How do we lower our resistance? Well, of course, this can be done by overexertion, too little sleep, or improper nourishment. But more often it is done with negative thinking.

Anxiety can cause tension headaches. Worry can cause ulcers. Heavy responsibilites can cause back troubles. The list is endless.

Self-mastery begins with your acceptance of yourself as boss of your body. If there is a morale problem in the shipping room of your factory, you would want to get to the cause of it. So it is with your body. What problems are causing you to "express" dis-ease?

A young man came to me with a problem he did not wish to take to a physician: He had warts on his anus. We sat and talked. I asked him what was on his mind most these days. He replied he was not getting along with his girl friend. They had both agreed it would be better if she went back home. However, each time he took her to the airport, he would return home later only to find she had changed her mind and was there waiting for him.

"How many times has this happened?" I asked him.

"About six," he replied.

"And how many warts do you have?"

"About six," he replied, smiling and beginning to see the light.

The next time he took her to the airport, put her on the plane, and stayed until the plane had taken off. He called me a week later and reported—no warts.

How well the problem fits its physical expression! He gives me a pain in the neck. She galls me. Oh, my aching back. These are expressions that can be both vocalized and physically manifested.

The metaphysician treats causes not symptoms. He knows that true causes are usually not physical, but in the climate of consciousness—if that climate is beset with clouds of vexation, inhibition, bitterness, animosity, impatience, resentment, anger, indignation, stubbornness, false pride, tension, sorrow, and disappointment.

In Chapter 4, I gave you the method the Hawaiian Kahunas used to get rid of unwanted negative attitudes and feelings. They relaxed, and commanded these unwanted negative attitudes to leave their bodies when they shook their right legs and their left legs.

If you have not done this exercise and you would like to prepare your own mental climate for better health, do it now. If there is some specific negativity that you are aware of, here is how to handle it.

Metaphysical Action Plan for Dissolving the Mental Cause of a Physical Problem

1. Review the situation that is presently causing a particular emotional stress.

2. Pick a word that expresses the positive opposite of this negative emotion. (*Example*: hate—love, anxiety—security, worry—confidence, impatience—patience, etc.)

3. Place a glass of water by your chair.

4. Relax. See yourself beset with the negative emotion. See the glass of water as containing the solution—filled with the opposite positive emotion.

5. Drink the water, knowing you are filling yourself with the positive emotion you need, and the negativity will leave you when you next urinate.

6. End session. Then urinate, feeling an exhilaration of positivity.

Enter the Cells of Your Body and Imbue Them with Youth and Radiance

With negativity removed, the error-causing factors in your internal health maker are removed and you are ready to use your metaphysical powers to turn up your life energy and roll back the years.

Your body is an organism. It is similar to an organization. You might say an organism is an organization of cells. Have you ever visited a large company engaged in the production of some product? It has many divisions and departments. These are connected by servicing and communications activities. So it is with the body.

Some years ago a large electronics firm was experimenting with different shades of fluorescent lighting to see what effect these colors might have on the rate of production. When they switched to a slightly blue light, production went up. When they switched to a yellow light, production also went up. When they switched to any other kind of light, production went up.

The engineers then realized that the workers were not reacting to the color of the light, but to the fact that somebody was paying attention to them. Morale and production rose when they felt that somebody cared.

At the start of this chapter, I told you how Dr. Carl Simonton's patients accelerated their recoveries by "visiting" their blood streams. Health cells respond, too, by becoming healthier when your consciousness visits them in appreciation.

How long since you have visited your "factory" and acknowledged the good work going on? Probably never. Now is the time Then see how your entire body responds.

Metaphysical Action Plan for Heightening Your Youthful Vitality

1. Make a tape of the following instructions and play it back to yourself or else memorize the procedure (not necessarily word for word). Either way, perform it at your alpha level.

2. Turn your awareness to your scalp. Note the tiny pores. Make one of these pores very large. Even larger. You are now able to enter the pore. Inside you appear to be in a forest. These are your hair follicles. Walk up to one hair follicle. Greet it warmly. Thank it for a job well done in providing you with your crowning glory. Tell it to pass the good word on to all the hair cells of the body.

Move down to the inside of the skin of the face. Speak to some of the skin cells. Compliment them on the fine texture and radiance of your complexion. Give them a message of congratulations for all the skin cells of the body.

Now move your awareness into your lungs. What a fabulous job is being done here. Assure your lung cells that you are doing your best to provide them with pure air. Praise them for the great job they are doing in receiving oxygen for the bloodstream and expelling unwanted impurities.

Now enter the bloodstream from the lungs and travel along with the blood expressing admiration to all the corpuscles and plasma cells for the splendid job they are doing in feeding the cells of the body and protecting the whole system from foreign intruders.

As the blood enters the heart, stop off there for a tip of

the hat to all of the four chambers of the heart and the valves. Thank them for their around the clock supplying of blood pressure and beautiful timing and control. Feel love for all of your heart cells.

Now on to your stomach. Here is a wondrous chemical laboratory, indeed. Hardly a day goes by when new combinations of foods are not fed into the stomach, yet it always produces just the right digestive juices to do the job. A pat on the back to the stomach cells and all of its juice "suppliers" and intestinal tract all the way to the colon, for their fine work.

A special visit to the liver. Acknowledge to the liver cells the vital importance to the organization of the job they do. Perhaps you might want to award a certificate of achievement here or elsewhere in your visit.

Next, the kidneys. Shake hands with several kidney cells and have them express your gratitude to all the cells in that department for a job well done.

Now into the backbone. Remind the cells of the backbone how much the whole system depends on them and how all the bone cells deserve everybody's vote of thanks.

Finally, enter the leg muscles. Express your admiration for how well they carry their load. Have them pass on to all the muscle cells of the body your sincere thanks!

Before leaving the body at this point, turn around and salute all of the cells of the body, sending thoughts of love and rapport all the way down to the toes and up to the head.

3. End your session feeling a new peak of vitality.

How to Rid Yourself of the Aging Habit While Your Friends Move on in Years

The Bible predicts the end of sorrow and death. (Revelation 21:4—"And God shall wipe away all tears from their eyes; and there shall be no more death, neither sorrow, nor crying, neither shall there be any more pain.")

The metaphysician sees the Bible less literally, more as a symbolic record of the evolution of man's consciousness. Could it be that man will soon become aware that he is programming his own cells to age and die at the expected time? Could it be that, perhaps with the aid of modern science, man will realize his potential life span is certainly closer to Methuselah's nine hundred years?

Friend Stuart thinks so.

Stuart is the author of *How to Conquer Physical Death*.[1] He believes biological death can become obsolete as man conquers the concept of death in his individual consciousness. Many metaphysicians in the past have predicted this—Joel Goldsmith and Thomas Troward to name a couple.

People are constantly programming themselves to grow old. The metaphysician who reverses the mental programming makes decidedly observable progress on the physical level.

This is a herculean job, though. For every time you see a wrinkled, stooped shouldered, or a graying person you are counter-programming. Besides these exposures to aging people, there are many other little hammer blows every day that keep hitting home to us the fact that we will grow old and die. Here are just ten quick examples:

- Ads on how to get rid of wrinkles, blemishes, gray hair and other aging symptoms.
- The retirement, pension, Social Security syndrome.
- Activities involving the "golden years," senior citizens, and old people's homes.
- Grandparents and great grandparents—their place in the family.
- Interest in how old you are or how old he is.
- Cemetaries, funeral parlors, obituaries.
- Negative attitudes that cause aging tensions and sap youthful energy.
- Failures and disappointments that weaken the "will to live."
- Acceptance of several changes as signs of old age.
- Acceptance of other minor physical changes to reinforce the "I'm aging" concept.

A golfer who knows the power of positive thinking has an easy

[1]Friend Stuart, *How to Conquer Physical Death*, (San Marcos, California: The Dominican Press, 1968).

task insulating himself from negative influences compared to some-body who wishes to insulate himself from aging influences. The golfer just looks straight ahead, ignoring the rough on one side and the hazards on the other.

In a way, the metaphysician wishing to prolong youth needs to tread a similar mental path, albeit more narrow—a path of ignoring the sights and sounds of old age and of reinforcing the sights and sounds of youth.

How Bill P. Has Maintained a Youthful
Body and Mind into His Nineties

Bill P. was reminded of old age when his wife died some 30 years ago right on the actuarial statistical schedule. He decided that this was not going to be his "route." Already over 60 himself, he had been exercising, eating properly, and in other ways taking care of himself, so he still looked in his prime. He began associating with young people, dating young women, and living a youthful life. He used the affirmation method of correcting any aging programming the environ-ment threw at him by exclaiming daily, "Every day in every way, I am getting better and better, younger and younger, wiser and wiser." Today Bill P. is in his nineties, and he still looks like he's in his sixties—and is still popular with young women in their twenties.

Geriatrics, the study of aging, has been confined largely to biolog-ical functions. We are now on the threshhold of its shift to mental functioning. It should begin to make accelerated progress.

I do not profess to know where Ponce De Leon's Fountain of Youth is located. But I'll give odds it's not in Florida, Hawaii, or Hunsaland, but that it's in consciousness.

Whether the doorway to agelessness is through the alpha level of mind is also controversial. Gene Savoy, internationally known explorer, has studied the wisdom of lost civilizations and their special practices relative to the sun. He has founded the International Com-munity of Cosolargy to share this cosmic solar science, part of which is teaching the student to operate consciously at brain rhythms more than ten times as rapid than alpha.

What is certain is: We can dehypnotize ourselves from growing old for the reason that we are expected to grow old. We can program out the "grow old" conditionings and program in new conditionings conducive to youthful behavior. Here is how:

*Metaphysical
Action
Plan to
Program
Old Age
Out and
Youthfulness
In*

1. Relax deeply,
2. Affirm to yourself—either verbally or mentally: "My mind and body are perfect. The forces of aging have no control over me. I am ageless. I am master of my life."
3. See yourself as if in a mirror—youthful, enthusiastic, radiant, energetic, and healthy.
4. End relaxation, feeling as a child. Repeat daily.

How to Transform a Glass of Water into the Elixir of Life

Ponce De Leon knew that the secret of perpetual youth lay in water. He looked for a special kind of water. But the whole while that water was as close to him as the water he drank.

Water is the universal solvent. It washes away the poisons of our bodies, including the old cells that are being replaced by new cells.

Actually our body cannot grow old; only cells can grow old. And these cells are being replaced constantly. It has been estimated that in one year's time nearly every cell in our body has been replaced at least once.

The water we drink cleanses our body internally by ridding it of cell waste matter, including dead cells. Water is everywhere in our body. We are more water than we are anything else. Is it any wonder that we can live weeks without food but not without water?

Water can be used not only for survival but for youthful survival. It can be metaphysically charged to be your elixir of life. Here is how:

*Metaphysical
Action
Plan to
Transform
a Glass
of Water
Into an
Elixir of
Life*

1. Fill an amber colored vase or bottle with water. Cover it to keep out dust. Place it in the sun for several hours.
2. Fill a glass with this suncharged water. Hold it with the tips of the fingers of both hands so that the fingers are not touching each other.
3. Drink the water, sipping it slowly, projecting in to each sip the mental picture of yourself as a perpetually joyous, child-like person. Finish drinking the entire glass.
4. Relax. See yourself sipping this water again and again, and looking younger each time you do it
5. End the relaxation feeling recharged,

How to Project Health
Power to Other People Miles Away

Metaphysicians have found that it is easier to heal others of specific health problems than to heal themselves. One metaphysician often seeks the aid of another when his own health is involved. Healing yourself is like lifting yourself up by your bootstraps.

The key to self-healing in metaphysics is to remove the cause.

The key to healing others metaphysically is by removing the symptom.

The method is now simple for you:

Metaphysical   1. Relax deeply.
Action   2. Visualize the person vividly.
Plan to
Heal Others   3. Perform some "mechanical" act to correct the symptom.
    4. End relaxation, knowing correction is made.

Let me explain Step 3 by means of a few real life examples:

- A man has a stone in his kidney, or gall bladder. When you visualize him, see the stone as if you are seeing through his body. Take an imaginary pair of pliers and crush the stone. (This man passes the stone the next day.)
- A woman is having coughing spells. Her doctor advises giving up smoking. When you visualize her, see the dark areas on her lungs. Use a solvent in an imaginary spray can to dissolve the material that causes the dark area. (This woman's cough diminished immediately. But she continued to smoke and the condition returned.)
- A man is having hiccup attacks every seven days like clockwork. Each attack lasts about 24 hours. See this man helping this condition every time he drinks water. The attacks become of shorter duration and the time between them is longer. (This is exactly what took place until the hiccups were no longer a problem.)

Miss Rita C.'s Dancing
Career Survived Her Tumors

Miss Rita C. had two tumors in the area of her uterus. Her physician treated her for pain as they grew bigger. A belly dancer by profession, she became more and more incapacitated by periods of severe pain and discomfort. She told me of the trouble and invited my help as she feared the possible complications and disfigurement of surgery.

Once a day for two weeks, I went to my alpha level, pictured Rita, entered her body by the most logical route, bringing with me an imaginary spray can. This spray shrank tumors. I saw the tumors, one on the left and one on the right. I sprayed them both. Each time I returned, the tumors appeared smaller to me.

Part way along the two week period, Rita called me. "I have no pain. Whatever you are doing is good."

At the end of the two weeks, her physician reported the tumors had regressed to a fraction of their former size. To this writing, over a year later, the tumors have caused Rita no further trouble.

You do not have to possess a knowledge of anatomy to do this metaphysical healing work. Just as the patients were instructed by Dr. Simonton to visualize their bloodstreams doing its work in any way they wished, so you can proceed with your health corrections at a distance in any way you wish.

It is the *concept* of correction that does the metaphysical work.

Critical cases, such as so-called terminal cancer, are unpredictable. For instance, a nationally known songstress came to a metaphysical healing session held at the author's house. She put the name of a friend of hers into that evening's metaphysical action plan. The person was in a local hospital where the doctors called his condition the last stages of cancer.

The following day that person called from the hospital and asked how she was. "How am *I*?" she replied stunned. "How are *you*?"

"Oh, I feel great. I'd like to get out of this place."

The next day he was out, taking a drive with his family.

On the other hand, a New York couple visiting Hawaii placed the wife's father in the metaphysical healing session. He was also called a terminal cancer case and had been in pain for some time. Three hours after the session, he passed on.

"Healing" can be in two directions. In each, the universal will is done. The person returns to good health—or, from whence he came.

Hundreds of thousands of people in all walks of life have learned how to relax, to Alpha Picture, then to detect and correct abnormalities, at a distance, in people they are asked by their friends to help. Silva Mind Control, founded by Jose Silva in the past decade and headquartered in Laredo, Texas, teaches this in some forty hours of training.

How a Grandmother Saved Her Grandson

A three-year-old boy was near death. His kidneys were not functioning properly and his little body was puffed with toxins. His young mother did not seem to care and left the youngster with her own mother most of the time. The doctor was administering cortisone, a powerful drug which alleviated the condition but admittedly would have fatal side effects.

The grandmother decided to use metaphysical means to ascertain both the cause and the cure. At her alpha level, she saw the boy become bloated as he drank milk. She mentally "filtered" poisons from his blood. When she ended her metaphysical work, she followed through and kept him off milk. The results were immediate. He cried less, played more. His bloat was reduced. She purposely missed a doctor's appointment, but took him the following week. The doctor noted the boy's improvement but still administered cortisone.

Feeling that the medical cure might now be more dangerous than the disease, the grandmother kept up her metaphysical treatment without further visits to the doctor. Except for relapses, especially when the young mother gave the child milk, the boy improved steadily.

"Miracles" happen when you project a picture of perfect health to a person. Mary Baker Eddy, founder of Christian Science, understood and taught this. She saw that anything short of perfection had a cause in consciousness. Correct that imperfection in consciousness and it disappeared in the material world.

These fundamentals of metaphysical healing are also understood by Unity Churches throughout the United States (headquarters—Lee's Summit, Missouri) and are being taught by the Church of Religious Science founded by Ernest Holmes.

Let me repeat a previous warning. State laws forbid medical or healing practices without a license. However, metaphysical healing at a distance is spiritual healing. To stay within the law, do not diagnose and do not perform metaphysical healing when a person is in your presence.

How to Get Immediate Relief from Pain

In the early chapters of this book, I gave you the method for creating numbness in your hand and passing that numbness on to a painful part of your body for temporary relief.

There is a metaphysical method for doing this on a somewhat more permanent basis. However, remember that where pain persists, see your doctor. Pain is a signal that there is a problem that needs to be corrected.

This method is not correction. It is the removal of pain from an objective to a subjective level. When pain is at its usual objective level, it is objectionable. When you move it to your subjective level, it becomes subject to your removal.

Metaphysical Action Plan for Relief of Pain

1. You are about to ask yourself a series of questions that appear unreasonable on the surface. But resolve now that you will answer them as accurately as you can.
2. Relax.
3. Point to the exact location of the pain.
4. Ask yourself, "If this pain could fit a container, what shape container would it need?" (Cup, pan, pitcher, bucket, etc.)
5. Ask yourself, "If this pain had a color, what color would it be?" (Red, orange, gray, brown, etc.)
6. Ask yourself, "If this pain had a taste, what might that taste be?" (Sweet, sour, bitter, bland, etc.)
7. Ask yourself, "If this pain had a smell, what might that smell be?"
8. Again, point to your pain, noting that it has moved slightly.
9. Repeat 4, 5, 6, and 7, noting that the shape, color, taste and smell have changed.
10. Again, point to your pain. Repeat several times until you can no longer point to pain because it is gone.
11. If pain has moved in a certain direction but has not quite left your body, place it in the container it will fit and move it a foot outside your body and command it to stay out.
12. End relaxation, pain free.

How Mrs. Betsy Y. Got Rid of a Nagging Lower Backache in Three Minutes

I was giving the aforementioned instructions to a class at the University of Hawaii when a woman raised her hand and asked whether I might demonstrate on her as she had a backache that had been bothering her for quite a while. She came to the head of the room, sat in a chair, relaxed, and I asked her the questions. She pointed to the pain. It fit a pot, was black, tasted bitter, and smelled acrid. Then it moved lower, fit a cup, was gray, and had no taste or smell. The third try found her unable to locate the pain. She reported to the class several days later that the pain had not returned.

I have found this method to be successful throughout a variety of pains—headache, menstrual cramps, and even the pain of a healing wound. You can ask these questions of other people to help themselves as there is no touching, diagnosing, or treating involved. But you will be doing them more good if you teach them to do this for themselves, without you.

Ten Metaphysical Commandments
for Maintaining Perfect Health

Cause is in consciousness—the unseen.

Effect is in circumstances—the seen.

When the effect is in circumstances involving health, you can be sure that your consciousness is causing this. But how?

The key is in negativity.

Here are ten major areas where you are likely to find negativity entering your consciousness. Convert this negativity to positivity and you create a consciousness of continued good health:

1. Accept criticism as the other person's problem, not yours.
2. Appreciate yourself and reaffirm your self-worth whenever necessary.
3. See the good points in circumstances. See even problems as happening for the best.
4. Rather than looking backward with sorrow, look forward with joyous expectation.
5. Rather than fret about what you do not have, appreciate what you have.
6. Learn from mistakes, so that you can convert them into triumphs.
7. Insulate yourself from distasteful surroundings through wholesome detachment.
8. Let go readily of what you no longer need and make the most of what you now attract.
9. Grow in courage and self-mastery from every circumstance.

10. Be aware of the larger Consciousness of which you are part.

These might be called the ten metaphysical commandments to good health. They are beyond the physical—in the unseen world of consciousness.

Observe them. And enjoy perfect health.

Positively.

8

Know Other People's Thoughts and Feelings Even Miles Away –Through Miracle Metaphysics

It has now been proven that plants can know people's thoughts and inner feelings. If a woman fibs about her age, a polygraph connected to a plant will register a definite reaction by the plant. When she tells the truth about her age, no such plant reaction occurs.

If the owner of a plant is on a trip, the plant registers the tension of plane takeoff or landing and other mental stresses even thousands of miles away.

Are plants more advanced than humans? I think not. It is just that humans are so "smart" they know they cannot do this.

I remember seeing a sign in an executive's office. It read something like this:

We humans outsmart ourselves.

We know we cannot see auras, so we don't.

We know we cannot control pain, so we take a pill.

We know we cannot affect our luck, so we accept it, good or bad.

We know we cannot influence other people at a distance, so we go to see them and argue.

We know we cannot enjoy abundance honestly without sweat and tears, so we slave for it.

And we know we cannot pick up information at a distance, so we write a letter or make a phone call.

Meanwhile, a dog lost on a trip hundreds of miles from home, scratches on the front door two weeks later. Birds stop singing before an earthquake strikes. And ants swarm to an open honey jar a quarter of a mile from their hole in the ground.

Stupid plants. Stupid animals.

The Man Who Talked to Plants and Learned Their Secrets

George Washington Carver, descended from a Negro slave, became one of America's greatest agricultural chemists. He attributed this to his talking to plants. By asking the peanut, "Why did the Lord make you?" Carver seemed to be told, "Work on me with temperature and pressure." He soon had developed a score of valuable uses for the then lowly peanut, and proved to local farmers that they could profit by planting peanuts instead of soil-depleting cotton. The sweet potato "talked" to him, too, and "told" him of many uses. You can find out the secrets of plants, he would explain, if you love them enough.

Parlor Games That Demonstrate Thought Transference

Thought transference is taking place between you and others constantly. Once you are alerted to this fact you begin to notice it happening more frequently.

For instance, watch a person walk by on the street. "Tell" him, by thinking, that his nose itches. Then see if he brushes it with his finger. Many will.

Or, have a group of friends decide on an object in the room while a volunteer waits outside. He is called back as everyone thinks or visualizes the object. The number of times such a volunteer walks right up to the object is impressive.

A falling game, mentioned before, is also interesting. A volunteer leaves the room as the others form a circle and decide who in the circle is "it." The volunteer is called back, enters the circle, closes his eyes, turns around slowly until he feels the urge to fall backwards—usually into the arms of "it." The success of this game depends upon how well the members of the circle were visualizing him doing just that—with their eyes open.

A deck of ordinary playing cards affords more opportunities for testing thought transference. One person might examine a selection of 20 cards (evenly divided black and red) one by one as the second person "guesses" the color. Any "hits" over ten, produced consistently, is evidence of thought transference.

For years, opponents of the concept of telepathy have argued that body language is the tip off, but this card game will be just as effective if the two parties are back to back. Similar precautions can be taken in other ESP games to remove any possible visual effects.

One element is missing in games that operates in real life. It is the factor of urgency. ESP needs this factor in order to get through the screen that protects us from other people's thoughts. Even in real life, with urgency, it operates more effectively with pictured thoughts at the *alpha* level of mind.

The Key to Mental Communication at a Distance

The scene is Maimonides Medical Center in New York. A man is sleeping. When biofeedback instruments indicate he is in a dream phase, a staff member selects a piece of artwork from a stack at random and focuses his attention on it. Then he awakens the man and requests a report on his dream. Later, a team of judges examine the painting and the transcribed report by the dreamer and agree that there is a positive correlation between the two.

The scene shifts. A mother in a Detroit suburb is playing bridge one evening at a friend's house two miles from her own. When she is dummy, she leaves the bridge table and relaxes in an armchair. The other three are too busy playing out the hand to notice that she has closed her eyes and appears to be dozing.

She is not dozing. She is at her alpha level and is picturing her six-year-old boy, sleeping back at her house. She talks to him at the mental level.

"David, when you have to urinate, wake up and go to the bathroom. You will feel much better sleeping in a dry bed and mother will be much happier in the morning."

The bed-wetter goes to the bathroom that night. A few more nocturnal "conversations" by his mother and David is no longer a bed-wetter.

Note that there were two factors here contributing to successful communications at a distance: The sender was at a relaxed alpha level. The receiver was at a relaxed level of mind, too—probably deeper than alpha.

Common to both was silence. The mother was able to turn off the sounds of the card players as she relaxed. The boy was totally oblivious to any sounds that may have been audible in his bedroom.

This silence is unique to us. We seldom experience it. The waking day is a compendium of sights, sounds, tastes, touches, and smells. These cut off the tiny ESP impulses that would otherwise come through "loud" and clear as they do to the birds, insects and other wildlife.

The key to mental communication at a distance is silence. You, as a successful metaphysician, need to know about four basic levels of silence:

Level 1. The sounds of the environment are hushed, like at dusk. You enjoy "listening" to this kind of *natural silence*.

Level 2. The body and mind are relaxed. Outside sounds do not disturb this silence. You are lost in thought and in mind imagery. This is your *alpha silence*.

Level 3. The body and mind are relaxed but there is no picturing, no thinking actively. Time and space recede. Pure inspiration and attunement take place in this *deep silence*.

Level 4. You have reached your innermost center where dwells the Absolute. There is only spacelessness and timelessness. You may stand at the threshhold but never quite enter the *Absolute Silence*.

Communication mentally takes place at Level 2 and Level 3. Transmission of messages to others, such as the mother to her bed-wetting son, takes place at Level 2. Reception of messages from others, or the tapping of other people's thoughts, takes place at Level 3.

Since you have already learned to go to your alpha level of mind and to enjoy the alpha silence, you already know how to send messages to others. We will go into more detail about this in a moment.

However, the deep silence, required for tapping the thoughts of others, involves methodology new to you. We will spell this out later in this chapter.

How to Get the Metaphysical
Ear of Persons You Need to Contact

In previous chapters, we discussed how a piece of clothing or a picture can be used to "reach" a person you want to attract to your side.

This is also useful in communicating your thoughts to a person, but it is a kindergarten technique once you have the ability to visualize clearly and see the person distinctly with your eyes closed and relaxed. Alpha Picturing the person connects you instantly just like automatic direct dailing.

However, the line may be busy.

Messages do not get through as easily if the person you wish to reach is in a highly active state—busy at work, socializing at a party, or traveling here and there.

High voltage messages may still get through. Urgent messages of calamity or dire need will penetrate the busiest of minds.

But it is best to do your Alpha Picturing at a time when you know the person is likely to be quietly at home. Here are some optimum times:

- When a person is watching television.
- When a person is about to fall asleep.
- When a person has just awakened.
- When a person is sleeping (the message comes in dream form).
- When a person has had one or two alcoholic drinks.
- When a woman is having her menstrual cycle.
- When a man or woman has just finished making love.

In the case of radio or television, the music must be harmonious rather than of the hard rock type and the program must be absorbing rather than exciting. Many people go to deep alpha in such cases. Of course, just falling asleep or just awakening is the best bet, though not easy to time.

Alcohol is a depressant and relaxes the person, but it also desensitizes. One ounce of 100 proof liquor might desensitize a 100-pound person more than two such drinks might affect a 200-pound person.

Completion of the act of love yields a euphoric relaxation replete with alpha. Women are more suggestible and subject to "control" through mental messages during their monthly period.

These are receptive situations because they come closest to the alpha silence and the deep silence. In the next chapter, we will learn how to transcend the need to have the receiver at a receptive state using special charms, spells, and mantras; meanwhile, here is how to proceed with a message:

Metaphysical Action Plan to Send a Message to a Person Wherever That Person Is

1. Relax deeply and picture the person.

2. If the person is visualized in some activity or if the picture is in some way symbolic of activity, end your relaxation and try at some later time. If the picture is a quiet one, proceed to visualize your message as follows.

3. Visualize the person conforming to your request; or, visualize the situation you want that person to know about.

4. Next, see yourself writing the message in script on a pad with the person waiting for it.

5. Stamp the message URGENT. Hand the paper to the person.

6. End your relaxation, knowing the message has been received.

You Can Put Another Person's Head on yours and Know How They Feel and Think

If another person sends to you, you will receive especially clearly now that you have become psychically "sensitive." You will not have to know that the person is "sending" to you. You will not have to be at your alpha level or in the "silence." You will get the thought "out of a clear sky."

However, suppose that person is not "sending" to you. Can you tap in on them anyhow? You certainly can. Here is how one man did it.

How Bob A. Knew She Would Return and She Did

Bob A. was constantly bickering with the girl who lived with him. He thought he loved her. He kept asking her if she loved him. Neither would make this emotional commitment to the other.

Then one day, after a particularly bitter exchange, she left him.

Bob was literally beside himself. He could not sleep without her. The days were empty. I knew the answer but I wanted him to discover it for himself. I taught him Alpha Picturing. Then while he was imaging her, I asked him to reach forward with his hands and put her head over his like a helmet. His hands reached out, he moved them back over his head and gradually a smile came over his face. "Tomorrow!" he exclaimed. "She says she'll be back tomorrow."

At that moment, Bob felt as if he was his girl friend. He felt, "I've punished him enough. I'll go back to him first thing tomorrow."

She rang the doorbell at 10:30 a.m.

There is need for caution in performing the metaphysical act of putting on another person's head. If that person is in great emotional stress, physical pain, or upheaval of any sort, the experience can be a severely unpleasant one for you. So . . .

Warning: Be ready to remove the other person's head instantly as you put it on. At the first sign of a heavy weight on your head, a pain, or any uncomfortable thoughts or sensations, reverse the process, removing the head from yours and restoring it to the shoulders of its owner.

Metaphysical Action Plan for "Listening" to Another Person's Thoughts and Feeling His Emotions

1. Relax and picture the person.
2. Reach your hands forward and turn the person around so the back is to you.
3. Reach up to the head, lift it off and place it over your head like a helmet.
4. Accept any thought or feeling that comes to you as belonging to that person and being dominant in that person at that time. Return the head.
5. If there is a question still unanswered, turn the person around facing you, ask the specific question, and repeat steps 2, 3, and 4.
6. End your relaxation, the wiser.

Astral Travel, Soul Travel, and the Projection of Consciousness

What you have just done is neither astral travel nor soul travel. Astral travel involves the use of a level of body rather than a level of mind. It is an energy body that can leave the denser physical body asleep and physically travel at great speeds to other worlds.

Astral travel is living dangerously when you embark on it of your own volition. When it happens automatically, you are protected. I have never learned astral traveling, although I have no doubt that I have traveled astrally to other planes for some universal purpose that I may one day be aware of. I do not intend ever to learn it. The so-called astral body does not transcend space and time and so must consume time in traveling from here to there. For this reason the metaphysician prefers the projection of consciousness—instantly.

I can safely project my consciousness to wherever I wish and retrieve any information that is necessary to solve a human problem—mine or someone else's—so why go into other methods?

Soul travel is another method. I have no doubt that it is done and done effectively. Soul travel is more like what we are doing. It is the movement of the entire consciousness—the state of consciousness—rather than just the mental consciousness. This is called the soul body and when it reaches the soul alone, it has the apparent ability of being in all places at the same time.

The picturing faculty of the mind is an easy way to travel. It is like a television set—with it you go anywhere in the comfort of your own home.

When you see an image of another person miles away, you have projected a mental energy of consciousness which "sees" at a distance. What it "sees" then appears on what you might call the television screen of the mind.

What a fantastic apparatus to have once you know how to use it! The tube never needs to be replaced. It uses no electricity. There are any number of channels to tune to. And it is safe to use.

For many people who have difficulty visualizing in detail or distinctly, the television technique is an effective substitute. You follow the same procedures as previously given. But when you first relax with your eyes closed, you "see" a television set in front of you. Imagine that you have selected the person you are "tapping" as the channel you want. Then wait. A picture will arrive.

It will be that person.

How to Create a Magic Mirror
to See What is Happening Hundreds of Miles Away

Throughout the ages, men have been devising ways to help the average person to relax and picture.

The Hindus of India are especially adept at inducing this relaxation, and have been for centuries. Fakirs permit themselves to be literally buried alive and, by slowing their body processes, can survive for dramatically long periods.

Some swamis have gone so deep into the silence that their projection of consciousness comes through so vividly they are actually seen by the people they project to. This phenomenon of being seen in two places at the same time is also common in Africa's Nigeria.

Before the telegraph and wireless, it took six weeks for the news of Napoleon's defeat at Moscow to reach Paris, but it took only a few hours for details of the battle of Maineaud, hundreds of miles away and across high mountain ranges, to reach the market places of Calcutta.

The key to the Hindus' total relaxation is the magic mirror. You can use any kind of a mirror or polished surface. Hindus use crystal balls. These are expensive but well worth the investment. If not available to you, use a hand mirror, shaving mirror, or any small portable mirror.

First, you must perform a metaphysical act known as "changing" the mirror. Then, you will be able to see whomever you wish in the mirror without having to go through this step again.

In this chapter, we will confine ourselves to seeing that person in the present. In the final chapter of this book, you will learn how to use your charged up crystal ball or magic mirror to see the future.

Metaphysical Action Plan to Create a Magic Mirror

1. Place the crystal ball or mirror in front of you as you relax.

2. See yourself surrounded in light. It is a white light that penetrates your every pore. Breathe it in. Soak it up. Now project it to the mirror. See the mirror bathed in the white light. See the light penetrating into every molecule of the mirror.

3. Feel yourself surrounded with life energy, the energy of consciousness. A consciousness larger than yours fills the room. It is the consciousness of which your consciousness is part. It is a good feeling. Send the good feeling of this life energy to the mirror. Surround it with this life energy.

4. Now be aware of another kind of energy. It is higher in vibration than that light energy, so it is invisible. It is known as *akasha*—the light that gives birth to light. "See" this invisible light of all knowing surrounding you, filling you.

5. Project it to the mirror. Move your consciousness

with it so that you picture you are entering the mirror
with it.

6. Return your consciousness to your body. End your
   relaxation, feeling an exhilaration from the energizing
   experience.

Crystal ball or simple mirror, it is now a very special crystal ball
and what you might easily call your magic mirror. With it, you can
turn off your inner world and see anywhere you wish in the outer
world.

At best, relaxation methods are superficial. Regardless of how
deeply relaxed you feel, the vicissitudes of modern living still are
throbbing in your breast, being merely pushed aside temporarily by the
mind. By looking into this charged up mirror, you become more insu-
lated from these tensions. You are "taken out" of them. And so you
behave more efficiently as a metaphysician.

As you become more and more proficient in "seeing" when you
relax before your magic mirror, the entire knowledge of the universe is
yours to tap. You can be said to "read" the Akashic records—the
"memory" banks of the universe, and to transcend time as you view
the future events.

Here are some of its practical uses:

● To read the thoughts of persons anywhere on the face of the earth.

● To tune into what is happening anywhere at the moment.

● To recapture past events to help solve a problem or a crime.

● To help to heal persons at a distance.

● To contact persons who have passed on.

How Victor S. Found a Job with the Crystal Ball

Victor S. had purchased a six-inch crystal ball, charged it up, and
had many "curious" successes with it. However, Victor was now
without a job and he and I were discussing the problem. I recommended he ask the crystal ball to show him where his job might be
found. He saw a large hotel parking entrance in the crystal ball, recognized it, went over there immediately, and landed a job as a parking
manager. The vacancy had occurred only a few hours before.

How to Use the Magic Mirror
or Crystal Ball to Look into Someone Else's Life

Reading another person's thoughts a thousand miles away is duck soup once you have a charged up mirror or crystal ball.

Here is the procedure:

Metaphysical Action Plan for Tuning into a Person's Thoughts Miles Away Using the Magic Mirror

1. Dim the lights. Relax with the mirror positioned so you can see its entire surface but are *not* able to see your own face reflected.

2. Gaze into the mirror. Let your eyes focus either in front of the mirror or behind it but not on it.

3. Permit the mirror to cause you to drift into a sense of phantasy.

4. If you are seeking intellectual knowledge, see the mirror in a yellow light; for love matters—use a blue light. "Manufacture" this light with your imaging mind.

5. Search for the person in the mirror. Expect to see a scene in the mirror. Also expect to receive thoughts in your mind.

6. Phantasy may come first. Permit it to play itself out. Expect to see the person your are tuning into.

7. When the person is there, thoughts will come to your mind. They are the person's thoughts.

8. When satisfied, put the mirror down or cover the crystal ball. End your relaxation in the usual way and turn the lights back up.

The magic mirror and crystal ball are sophisticated metaphysical tools.

Actually, you are using an extension of your mind called the superconsciousness. It is the part of consciousness that connects you with the consciousness of the universe, sometimes called the Infinite Mind, the Infinite Intelligence, the Absolute, or God.

When used to solve human problems, it contributes to happiness and success. When used to create human problems, it backfires with misinformation and tends to produce unhappiness and failure.

Examples of proper use might be to:

- Know what an estranged loved one is thinking.
- Check on an absent child.
- Tap the thoughts of a suspected enemy.
- Predict the moves against you of a competitor.
- Determine whether someone is with you or against you.

Of course, there are hundreds of more valid, positive, constructive, creative uses. You, as a metaphysician, can now transcend the limits of your scalp and project your consciousness to the minds of others to bring your life to a higher and higher level of happiness, effectiveness, and success.

9

You Can Control Other People's Thoughts and Feelings

There is a saying among political campaigners that you can only change one percent of the minds. So most political activity is aimed at those minds that are undecided. However, those who know the techniques are able to control other people's thoughts. It has been going on for centuries.

I am not talking about "thought control" in its brainwashing sense. Prisoners of war have been inhumanly tortured to think the ways their captors want them to. False confessions have been wrung out of minds crazed by pain. However, *metaphysical thought influencing* is painless. It involves no discomfort. It usually happens even without the subject knowing it.

How Mr. W.S. Got Himself Transferred to the Day Shift

Mr. W.S. was on the night shift of a commercial cleaning company that worked in offices and office buildings. When he married, however, this schedule interfered with his family life. He requested a change to the day shift but his boss adamantly refused, pointing out that it would not be fair to one of the other workers to force him to shift.

Mr. W.S. brought a camera to work one night and stayed on until the day shift arrived. He playfully took a picture of them waiting for the company truck. When he developed the picture, he went to work on it in a special way: He relaxed, imagined he was there with them as he was when he took the picture. He pleaded his case. He suggested that one of them might have more free time during the day if he requested the night shift. He gave other advantages. He timed these little daily "talks" with them so that they occured just as the men were starting work—the time the picture was taken.

Meanwhile, he reminded his boss that, should there be a request for a transfer from day to night shift, he was available to make the opposite move. Inside of one week, it happened. A man in the picture asked for the night shift and Mr. W.S. got his spot on the day shift.

Your Consciousness Has a Wide Radius of Influence

A Soviet woman, Mrs. Nelya Mikhailova, has the ability to move objects at a distance, according to competent scientists and reliable reporters.[1] She has been seen to move cigarettes across a table, have a piece of bread move across a tablecloth and jump into her mouth, and separate the white of an egg from its yolk—all with the power of her mind.

Russian scientists have measured a magnetic field around Nelya ten times stronger than the earth's magnetic field, and also a strong electrostatic field. These, and other energies, seem to focus in tune with her eyes. As she stares, the object, even if nonmagnetic, acts as if it is magnetic. *Result:* her will power, transmitted through the energy of consciousness, manifests itself as physical energy.

Your consciousness—right this minute—has this power, too. You may not be able to move large objects with it, but molecules are certainly affected by it. Take the cells of your body. They respond to your thoughts quite dramatically as people with tension headaches, worry ulcers, and other psychosomatic symptoms well know.

But this radius of influence goes far beyond objects on a table or cells of your body. When on the mental or thought level, space is not a factor.

- You can mentally influence a child in the next room.
- You can mentally influence a person in a nearby house.
- You can mentally influence somebody a mile away.
- You can mentally influence a friend a thousand miles away.

[1]S. Ostrander and L. Schroeder, *Psychic Discoveries Behind the Iron Curtain,* (Englewood Cliffs, N.J.: Prentice-Hall, Inc., 1970).

● You can mentally influence a loved one anywhere on this planet.

Notice that I have used the words "friend" and "loved one" for the longer distances. The closer somebody is to you the better your mental "connection."

Psychic Magazine (October, 1974) reported that award-winning actress Cicely Tyson knew when her boyfriend was dating another girl. It did not matter how far away she was, she was able to tell him the details. These eventually disturbed him so much that he was convinced she was spying on him and he soon became her ex-boyfriend.

Could Miss Tyson have influenced her boyfriend to end his date prematurely? Could she have influenced him not to date in the first place?

Yes and no. Yes, if she knew the techniques and went about her mental work in a reasonable and logical vein. No, if she tried to impose her own selfish wishes on him without thinking of his needs.

This latter can work, too. But it is metaphysical "brainwashing." It takes longer and it goes against nature. Also, who wants a brainwashed lover?

So here we have the two factors for success in influencing other people:

1. The closer the person is to us emotionally, the greater the distance over which our metaphysical influence can be effective.

2. The more reasonable our approach, the more likely that our metaphysical influence will be accepted by the subject.

The late Richard Prentice Ettinger, co-founder and chairman of the board of Prentice-Hall, spoke at many sales meetings throughout the country and often told the story of how he went to see Ken Murray's successful show *Blackouts* in California.

Fascinated by a unique parakeet act in which an entire skit is performed by the colorful birds, Mr. Ettinger later went backstage to meet the birds' trainer.

"How did you ever get to train those birds to do their amazing act?" he asked.

"It was easy," replied the man. "All I had to do was think the way the birds think."

And that is the secret of successful salesmanship. You must put yourself in your customer's shoes.

It is also the way to induce other people to "buy" your way of thinking.

Five Rules That Help You
Win a Metaphysical Argument

You know how to relax and project your consciousness to another person by mentally picturing that person. You can sense his or her thoughts and feelings. But do you know how to influence those thoughts and feelings?

How Mr. L.L. "Influenced" the
Judge to Dismiss His Case

Mr. L.L. was present when police, stopping his car for speeding, found quantities of marijuana in the car and on the person of several occupants. Mr. L.L. did not know about the marijuana even though some was in the glove compartment.

A week before the trial was scheduled, Mr. L.L. began projecting this fact to the judge. He would visualize the judge not with hostility but with love. Then he would argue his case metaphysically, pointing out the facts.

When the hearing was held, the case against him was dismissed by the judge at the outset.

At the physical level all kinds of mental leverage can be used to successfully get your way—logic, justice, force, persuasion, threats, stress, duress. At the metaphysical level, there are also levers that help you get your way. But these are quite different.

If Mr. L.L. in this example could not feel love and understanding for the judge—if instead, he could only feel self-pity and antagonism toward the "system," he would not be able to "reach" the judge metaphysically.

Love is the telephone line that makes any metaphysical contact a *two-way* conversation. It is almost as if without love, the "telephone" does not ring at the other end.

Love is a primary rule that helps you win a metaphysical "argument." There are four more such basic rules.

Understanding is another. The more you understand the way a person believes, the more chance there is that that person will be receptive to understanding the way you believe.

Reason is a third. If a person is to be moved from where he stands to where you stand, he must have good reason. On a physical plane, good reason might be more money, more power, more benefits. However, on a metaphysical plane, reason is on a nonphysical level. Reason here must be on a mental level—that is, reasonable. Reason here means logic, equity, justice.

Need is a fourth. Human need adds the voltage to metaphysical communication. Need spells the difference between a request for cooperation and an S.O.S.

Rapport is the fifth basic element for influencing a person metaphysically. Rapport transcends love and understanding. It is the empathy that brings two people together, almost like a metaphysical glue. You bridge all separateness with rapport. You experience a oneness with that person no matter how great the physical distance between you.

Love. Understanding. Reason. Need. Rapport. All five need to be feelings within you. They cannot be synthetically created for the occasion. They must be sincerely felt.

How to Put the
Five Rules to Work for You

How do you "love" an adversary? How do you "understand" somebody whose ideas are diametrically opposed to yours? How can you feel a closeness with somebody who might even be your enemy? And how in the world can you be equitable and just when your need is pressing?

These are apparently contradictions. But not to the metaphysician.

You have seen yourself operate on a plane of apparent contradictions doing the metaphysical work in previous chapters—contradicting the laws of physics regarding space and time and communications. You have actually risen above these laws, by going into a mental level—a level where different laws operate, laws that might be quite opposite to physical laws.

Let me give you an example. You have experienced the pull of magnets. A magnet has two ends or poles. If you place the north pole of one magnet near the south pole of another magnet, the two are attracted to each other and pulled together. On the other hand, if you put the north end of each magnet together, they repel each other. On the physical level, opposites attract. Likes repel.

What about laws on the mental level? Are you attracted by people who are different than you? People who look different, dress differently, talk differently, think differently? Of course not. You prefer to be with people you can relate to, and you are more likely to prefer a member of the opposite sex (physical level) with whom you have common interests and beliefs (mental level).

So you temporarily shelve this physical plane in order to activate the five rules for winning an argument metaphysically—that is, convincing somebody miles away to see things your way.

Then you go to work on the mental plane. Here is how:

1. *Love*. Despite our physical differences, we are people. Despite our separateness, we are all parts of humanity: one man pollutes, all men suffer; one person is charitable, all people are elevated. See this common ground between the two of you. Ignore the differences; dwell on the brotherhood. If you take a moment to do this right now, you will get a warm feeling within a few seconds.

2. *Understanding*. You are the way you are because of your upbringing, learning, and environmental input. He is the way he is because of his upbringing, his learning, and his environmental input—all different from yours. If you have a right to be the way you are, does not he have the right to be the way he is? Take a moment now to feel his right to be as he is, to understand him.

3. *Reason*. Reason is a two-way street. First, see the reasonability of the other person's stand. It is not yours, it is his. Now mentally review the reasonability of your stand. There are pros and cons in each stand. Review how the pros minus the cons for your stand exceed the pros minus the cons for his stand. Become reason oriented to the problem.

4. *Need*. Think of your need in terms of how many problems could be solved if your need was met. How about secondary problems? When one problem is solved, usually others fade away, too. Involve as many people as you can in the chain of happiness that will result when your need is filled.

5. *Rapport*. Now permit all the positive feelings about this person to enter and to eclipse the feelings of hostility and antagonism. You are working together on this problem—on a higher level.

You are now ready to "move in" metaphysically and shift another person's feelings and attitudes in the direction you would like to see them move.

Metaphysical Action Plan to Win an Argument

1. Relax with a photo of the person. If no photo is available, a mental picture is fine.

2. Activate the five rules, as provided on the previous pages.

3. Ask the person to agree with you on the mental level now.

4. Open your eyes while still at the alpha level and look at the photo or see the person mentally—agreeing with you.

5. Review your five feelings of love, understanding, reason, need, and rapport.

6. End your relaxation, knowing that the differences are dissolved.

How Ralph G. Influenced His Father to Come to His Wedding

Ralph G. had a fist fight with his father at 16. Ever since then he and his father were barely polite to each other. After graduating from business college, Ralph got a job in computer programming and lived separately. Visits home were largely with his mother. If he dared more than a hello to his father, he would eventually find himself in an argument.

On one visit he brought his fiancee and announced their wedding date. His father was cold and noncommunicative. Later his mother called in tears saying his father would not come to the wedding. It was then that Ralph decided to use his metaphysical knowledge to gain his father's consent to come to the wedding and to resolve normal family relations.

In activating the five rules, he forgave his father for the events leading up to and including the fist fight. He pleaded his case mentally to his father, explaining how he, his wife, their future children, and his parents would all benefit from consenting. He ended his session knowing that the air had been cleared.

It was. His mother called up the next morning. "We'll both be there!"

How to Use Charms and Spells
to Have Other People Do Your Bidding

There is an old saying that if you wish to get a person of the opposite sex to say "yes" to your sexual desires, all you need to do is print in blood on three laurel leaves the names of the archangels— Gabriel, Michael, and Raphael. Place these leaves under his or her head or attach them in some way to a piece of clothing. Your wish then becomes their command.

Old wives' tale or truth?

Truth. Where consciousness goes, energy goes.

You are placing your conscious energy into living cells and adding saintly energy to boot. You are using blood to indicate it is a survival matter with you—that you cannot really live to the fullest without making love with that person.

The use of charms and spells are really the materialization into the "seen" of the metaphysical or "unseen."

It is easier for most people to go through the motions of inscribing three laurel leaves than activating those five rules. It is easier to trace Solomon's Seal and place it next to a person's picture than to exercise love, understanding, reason, and the feelings of need and rapport.

And it is not just physically easier. Expectation and belief are easier to come by. One may wonder if one is really projecting love, or feeling rapport, but there is no doubt that his photo is next to Solomon's Seal or that the laurel leaves are reposing under her bed. So charms and spells will continue to be useful metaphysical "tools" of consciousness. Here is how they work:

You read about a magic charm. Let's use the three laurel leaves as an example. Because it is called a charm, you place your faith in the leaves and expect them to work. This faith and expectation are like injection needles. They inject your consciousness into the leaves and into the end result.

The daughter of a female Hawaiian kahuna (metaphysician), who was noted for her miraculous healings, was occasionally asked by her mother to fetch certain herbs. The daughter could identify herbs growing in the forest but did not know just what ailments her kahuna mother was using each herb to heal. Occasionally her mother was away and somebody needed healing. She would tell the person to wait, fetch an herb, and apply the herb to the affected part or ask the person to make a tea of it. It did not seem to matter what herb she brought back for what ailment. It always worked. Today she is a respected, healing kahuna in her own right.

Consciousness runs the body. Consciousness creates disease. Consciousness heals it. Consciousness can harness an herb, giving that consciousness a vehicle to ride on. Such a vehicle is the charm or the spell.

I have given you in a previous chapter the procedure to use Solomon's Seal. Here now is a procedure to invest your consciousness in a charm to "get your way" with another person.

Metaphysical Action Plan to Use a Charm to Get Your Way with a Person

1. Find a white pebble or small stone. The smoother and whiter the better.

2. Place a white handkerchief over a small box and a large wad of cotton on top of the handkerchief. Set the stone in the cotton and position the box in a corner of a room. Focus a lamp with a white bulb so that it shines on the box.

3. Remove negative energies from the surroundings by standing, straddling the box back to the corner with a glass of water. Scatter drops of water with your right hand, starting at the left and thrusting the drops of water away from the corner, finishing at the right.

4. Sit on the floor in cross-legged fashion in front of the box, cotton, and stone, facing the corner.

5. Relax, close your eyes, and visualize the person doing your bidding, positioning your head in such a way so that, if you open your eyes, you are looking at the stone.

6. Bring into the picture you are visualizing a background mental picture of the stone, cotton, and box.

7. Open your eyes slowly, seeing the stone, but still maintaining your mental image of the person doing your bidding.

8. Close your eyes. End your relaxation, knowing the stone contains that visual image.

9. Place the stone as close as you can to the person— under the bed, under a piece of furniture, in the car, or even just on the grounds of that person's house or apartment.

10. From time to time in the days ahead, relax, and visualize the stone where you put it. See the stone radiating that "command" to the person.

It is dangerous metaphysical business to interfere wrongfully with
the freedom of choice of another person. This procedure will not work
if it is your intention to create a human problem or to do harm to
another person. There are built-in safeguards (including the author's
own metaphysical action plan to prevent injury to anyone).

However, this charm works beautifully to help solve problems
and to permit "ruts," obstacles, and habit patterns to be overcome in
the interests of progress. You may use it to influence a person to:

- Take a position which you know is more enlightened.
- Grant permission for something you need to do.
- Give you something that you should have.
- Read a book you feel that person should read.
- Say something to somebody you feel needs to be said.
- Sign a paper that should be rightfully signed.
- Pay a debt that should be paid.
- Grant a favor that would help you or others without creating prob-
  lems.
- Charge his mind from negative hostility to positive friendliness.

How to Use a Spell to Prevent
a Person from Acting in a Certain Way

A young woman called on me to help her solve a problem. She
was sure a jealous lover was interfering with her relationship with a
new boyfriend. She had had a "perfect" sexual relationship at the
outset but now it was not progressing to completion for her.

I searched her house and found a strange looking object. It was
nailed to the outside of her house just outside her bedroom window. I
took it down.

"Your old boyfriend knows some black magic," I explained.
"Everything will be all right now, but watch for more of his spells."

She called me the next day to confirm that "everything was as it
should be."

I don't believe in the use of black magic. I don't believe in the influencing of other people to do things that are against their will. I *do* believe in white magic. I *do* believe in influencing other people to change their will in a more positive, constructive, and beneficial direction.

I would be perfectly willing to give the young lady a counter-spell that would prevent the old boyfriend from attempting to interfere with her pleasure. But she did not ask me for it. In the next chapter, I give you some of these protective techniques.

Meanwhile, I will tell you how her old boyfriend created a spell that interfered with her sexual pleasure. I am not going to put this in the form of a metaphysical action plan, because I do not endorse such an abuse of metaphysical power.

Every object whether animate or inanimate has energy within it. A piece of string, metal, wood, or clay has a "spirit" of its own. Its molecules are in rapid motion or vibration and create an overall energy pattern unique to that object.

Knowing this, the metaphysician can use the five rules (love, understanding, reason, need, rapport) on an object just as if it were a person. By establishing these bonds with, say, a small stick, you can then instruct the stick to do your purpose. These instructions are carried out implicitly as soon as the stick, or other object used for the spell, is "planted,"—located near the person to be affected.

Warning: Negative acts of harm boomerang back to the perpetrator.

A Cosmic Law That You Need to Be Aware of in Controlling Others

I am being "controlled" in writing this book. I feel "right" about de-occulting certain secrets and hesitate to divulge others. You are being "controlled" in reading this book. You were moved to buy it and read it because it contains ways for you to solve life's problems.

Control is universal. Starting with our children, we all help to guide those with less experience or strength than we have. Indeed, there are higher energies operating on a different wave length than our energies that guide and assist us.

This control is an important factor in advanced metaphysics— advanced metaphysics, not because the exercise of this control is complicated, but on the contrary, it is quite simple. Advanced metaphysics because the exercise of this control is tied in with a cosmic law that makes the one that does the controlling quite involved in his own act.

You may, in fact, be sawing off the very limb you are sitting on.

This is the law of karma. It works just as surely as the law of gravity. As you sow, so shall you reap. The person who controls people by taking their arms while crossing a street, encouraging them when depressed, or enlightening them in areas of ignorance, is sure to feel cosmic reward. Similarly, control directed at harming a person in body or spirit is sure to lead to cosmic punishment.

There is no way to evade this law. There are no secrets from the universal consciousness of which yours and mine are part. There are no masks that can transform selfish motives into magnanimity. There are no excuses such as ignorance of good and evil. We are totally responsible for our controlling actions—physical or metaphysical.

End of my "Keep Out of the Reach of Children" instructions.

How to Get Instant Action from Others

There is not always time to create charms and spells. Situations arise that demand spur of the moment action on your part to get people to respond to your wishes.

Mrs. Theresa M. Won First Prize at the Garden Show

Rumors were flying around prior to the annual garden show that the judges were going to be partial to the mayor's wife. Mrs. Theresa M. was indignant. Her flower arrangements had always won honorable mention. This year she was out to get first prize. She could not let some other woman's "pull" interfere with justice. She relaxed. She saw the judges pause in front of her entry. She saw them leave. She saw them return with a blue ribbon. She won the blue ribbon. The mayor's wife got honorable mention.

Here is the "instant" metaphysical method for influencing others to do your bidding:

Metaphysical Action Plan for "Instant" Influence on Others

1. Go to a deep alpha level of relaxation.

2. Play the event in your imagination as you would like to see it happen. (Where possible, omit persons; instead, see the outcome as you want it to be.)

3. End relaxation, knowing the result is accomplished.

The whole process need take only a minute or less. It can be used at a distance or in the presence of the person(s) you wish to influence. Step 3 is important. Let there be no doubt in your mind that the deed is done.

It is.

10

How to Make Yourself Invulnerable to Psychic "Attack" by Enemies Known or Unknown

By now your are probably thinking, "If I can control other people, they can control me."

You're right.

And I had better go no further without giving you the means to protect yourself.

There are metaphysicians who use unscrupulous methods of controlling other people. They may get away with it for a while but it eventually boomerangs on them.

Take the Hawaiian death wish. It starts at the feet with paralysis that gradually engulfs the whole body. Death can come in less than a week. Kahunas (Hawaiian metaphysicians) had their practices, otherwise largely beneficent, declared illegal because of this kind of black magic. It was accomplished by making a pact with a newly departed soul still trapped between this dimension and the next.

I do not advocate taking the law into one's own hands. I do advocate your learning how to protect yourself from those who do.

How Mrs. Patricia A. Protected Herself from Gangsters

Mrs. Patricia A. owned a prosperous massage parlor. She had some fine masseuses working for her. One day three tough looking men walked in and sat down in her office as if they owned the place.

"From now on you're all working for us. We'll take the day's receipts and pay you well. We'll be like one big happy family. Anybody got any objections? If you do, you might be on the missing list tomorrow morning."

When she called me from a pay phone later to tell me what happened, Mrs. A. sounded half out of her mind with fright. "What can I do?" she pleaded.

I instructed her on the use of the white light. She must see her place of business surrounded in brilliant white light. It must *not* be a light of searing heat. Quite the contrary, it must be a light of intense love. Then she must see the three men, recalling their faces vividly, also bathed in her intense love light.

"Love them? How can I love them?" She hung up in tears. I put her on my mental screen to send her support and understanding.

A few days later the men returned. The business hours would be extended. Some of their own girls would be added to the staff "to make the men customers happy." More threats and . . ."We'll know about it if you call the police."

When Mrs. A. called to tell me about this second visit, she seemed more "in control." Yes, she could feel compassion for these misguided men. She would follow my instructions.

She did a splendid job with her metaphysical power, for the men never returned.

How to Use Light As an Impenetrable Psychic Shield

People who attack you on the physical plane are also attacking you on the mental plane. You might say the prime moving force—the cause—occurs on the mental level while the visible results—the effect—takes place on the physical plane.

Correct the cause on the mental plane and you protect yourself from effects on this physical plane.

Operating on the mental plane, rather than the physical plane, is the metaphysical approach. Its fundamental tool is *light*.

Mrs. Patricia A. used this tool. And it worked. It so happens that one of her masseuses knew the protective power of ti leaves. She placed them in and around the studio. And they worked. I will give you some of these protective charms, too, but these can be "de-fused" by an aware adversary.

Your light can not be turned off or interfered with. It protects you as an impenetrable shield. There is no power of darkness. There is only a power of light. Usually, "evil" or "devil" is associated with darkness. "Good" or "God" is associated with light. Darkness is not a source of power. Light is a source of power. So there is no such thing as the power of evil. Evil is just the absence of good.

Eleanor Roosevelt said, "It is better to light one candle than to curse the darkness." In metaphysics, we light up the sky.

Metaphysical
Action
Plan for
Creating a
Protective
Shield of
LIGHT

1. Relax, knowing you have nothing to fear from your enemies.

2. Visualize the room you are in as filled with bright sunlight. See the sunlight surrounding you with brilliance.

3. Create an imaginary rheostat. It brightens the light when you turn it clockwise.

4. Turn the rheostat clockwise. See the light getting whiter and more brilliant. Feel it as a warm protective love around you.

5. Turn back the rheostat to its original position. End your relaxation, feeling safer than you ever felt before. You are!

How Gregory B. Enlisted Higher
Energies to Come to His Aid

Gregory B. was a practicing metaphysician. He helped people free of charge. Another metaphysician came to town. He helped people for a fee of $100. When this newcomer heard of Gregory's beneficence, he tried to talk him out of it. "You are casting pearls before swine," he said. "Pearls, maybe," replied Gregory, "but swine, no."

Gregory then began to get recurrences of a sickness he thought he had conquered. Now no medicine helped, including his own metaphysical self-treatments. Then Gregory realized he was being "zapped" by this newcomer. He remembered a metaphysician he knew some years ago who had passed on. He visualized that person, as if he were alive, told him of the problem, promised to return the favor if needed. The next morning the sickness was gone and did not return.

A few weeks later the newcomer had left town.

How to Call on Higher
Energies for Help in Emergencies

In the above case, the newcomer metaphysician knew that Gregory B. had complete knowledge of the protective white light. So he merely "activated" a problem that was already inside Gregory—his old illness.

This is just one example of the many metaphysical devices that can be used to do harm. Once man invented the club, it was only a matter of time before he invented a protective stick. Then came the spear and the shield, the gun and armor plate.

In metaphysics, we deal with energy—the energy of consciousness. Sometimes we come up against metaphysical weapons that require a higher energy than our own consciousness to combat.

Gregory B. called on a higher energy—the conscious energy of a metaphysician on the other side. His was a higher energy not by dint of the fact that he was on the other side, but because of the metaphysical power and wisdom he had attained while alive.

Death does not breach the law of conservation of energy. The energy of consciousness survives. Recently, it has been discovered that simple cassettes can record "voices" from beyond. Prove this to yourself.

Metaphysical Action Plan to Pick Up Voices from Another Plane

1. Place a new cassette tape in the machine. Turn the volume all the way up. Switch on to record.

2. Remain in the room quietly. After about ten minutes say aloud, "I am now going to my alpha level and welcome communication via cassette."

3. Relax and turn your awareness to the ceiling, or a point just above your forehead.

4. After about ten more minutes, end your relaxation and turn off the cassette.

5. Rewind and play back at top volume or connect to stereo speaker for a volume gain. If voices are heard they may be hard to understand at first. With repeated playback, the ear will become more accustomed to the abnormal tonal quality.

The only value in hearing these voices is to confirm in your own mind that they are there. The cassette does not provide a two-way communication. You can only hear them—they, apparently, cannot respond to you. Furthermore, the conversations heard are seldom meaningful. They seem to be like people talking in their sleep.

To contact highly evolved energies you need to *know* they are there. Two-way communication again is not possible. You can send at will. Your sending set is your mind. The thoughts you send to high energies are received instantly.

If you send in doubt, their reaction is doubtful. If you send in disbelief, you are fed reinforcement for that disbelief. If you send in confidence, your confidence is rewarded—you receive an answer to your transmission. That answer comes in the form of guidance for you, or action through another person.

Here, then, is an effective way to protect yourself from psychic attack by your earthling enemies or rivals: You can call on Higher Authority for assistance.

Metaphysical Action Plan to Enlist Protection from Another Plane	1. Relax. Close your eyes.
	2. Send a psychic "S.O.S." Turning your eyes upward, call on all of the Higher Energies that your religion has taught you exist and others you have heard about. Include Jesus, Buddha, Mohammed, the Hierarchy of Angels, the Ascended Masters, the Saints—all by name to the extent that you know these names.
	3. Explain the problem. Ask for correction of the symptoms and protection from the outside cause.
	4. End your plea with thanks and open your eyes, knowing it is done.

How to Protect Yourself from Psychic "Vampires" That Suck Your Energy

Have you ever gone through a period of great lethargy, wondering why you do not have the energy you usually have? Or have you known somebody who went into the doldrums for long periods of time?

We all have our cycles of enthusiasm and despair, energy and lassitude, optimism and pessimism. But these cycles are normal only when they are of short duration, as a few hours or, at the very most, a few days.

When negative periods continue for a week or longer, there is a chance that a psychic "vampire" is at work.

A psychic "vampire" is a person near you or a departed soul who is penetrating your etheric or "shadow" body and stealing your vitality.

This person may be doing it quite unconsciously, as unconsciously as the departed soul. Conscious, purposeful "vampires" can be talked out of their parasitic behavior. Unconscious "vampires" present a more difficult problem.

C.W. Leadbeater, the theosophical authority of the early 1900's, recommended hypnotism as the only way to restore the elasticity of your "shadow" body, its normal condition that prevents energy-sucking penetration from the outside. He offered as the only alternative a stepped-up radiance and vitality, but even so the person could be depleted while asleep.

How Mrs. Mary C. Threw Off a Five Year Psychic Attack That Had Drained Her Vitality

Mrs. Mary C. thought it was her female change of life that brought on the period of lethargy. Once a popular socialite, she now stayed entirely in her apartment except for brief afternoon strolls.

When nearly five years had passed and, despite medical attention, she was still in a chronic state of weariness, disinterest, and depression, she appealed to the author for assistance. I discussed psychic vampires with her. Then I gave Mrs. C. hypnotic suggestions that she was now strengthening her etheric shell—that is, it was being restored to its original elasticity and could no longer be penetrated by energy-sucking entities on this or any other plane.

Within two weeks, Mrs. C. became her usual pleasant self. She began to travel to nearby resorts and within several months she went on a trip to Europe. She even had a love affair in Greece.

It could have been female change of life that placed Mrs. C. in the negative state that attracted the psychic vampire. Her first reaction to my metaphysical explanation was "Well, let the poor creature feed on me, whoever it is. At least, I'll be doing some good." This reflects her state of consciousness that seemed to invite what was happening.

However, if it happens to you don't be fooled into thinking you are giving some soul nourishment. As Leadbeater saw it, the psychic vampire invariably wastes the energy he robs from you. He is incapable of assimilating it, so it is dissipated and his thirst continues.

The following metaphysical action plan should be used whenever psychic energy-sucking is suspected. This could be any time there is a prolonged period of lassitude without medical explanation. You do not have to know who is the culprit or even if there is a culprit. Leaks in the etheric, or shadow body envelope can occur for other reasons.

If you have somebody familiar with hypnotic techniques, that person can help you relax in Step 1, visualize in Step 2, and then give you the hypnotic suggestion in Step 3. If such a person is not available, you can be your own hypnotist, making the process one of self-hypnotism.

Metaphysical Action Plan for Strengthening the Shadow Body to Prevent Energy-Sucking or Leakage

1. Relax thoroughly.

2. Visualize a shadow body around you. It is as if you were sitting inside someone bigger than yourself and identical to you.

3. Affirm the following or accept it as an instruction from your hypnotist: "I visualize my shadow body. I strengthen its protective skin. It is now like strong elastic. No entity may invade me. I am fully protected by the strengthened skin of my shadow body.

4. End session, feeling free and energized.

What to Do if You Are Your Own Unconscious Psychic Attacker

Some people are their own worst friend. Some are even their own enemy. And some are their own psychic attackers.

You are your own worst friend when you keep telling yourself, "I can't," instead of "I can"; when you put yourself down, and limit your accomplishments with a perpetually poor self-image. You are Mr. "What If?" Color yourself gray.

You are your own enemy when you keep visualizing the worst instead of the best. You are putting creative energy into problems and bringing them into fruition, instead of solutions. You are "Mr. Yes, But." Color yourself brown.

You are your own psychic attacker when you fear psychic attack. You are your own psychic attacker when you dwell on morbid possibilites; think of suicide, crime and murder; or take drugs to escape. You are "Mr. No Way Out." Color yourself black.

You can tell who among your friends are their own psychic attackers. They bring the conversation around to financial crises, atomic war, or earthquake. If *The Exorcist* is playing in the next town, they'll drive the twenty miles to see it, even though they have seen it three times already. They are the Chicken Littles, ever warning that the sky is falling.

Psychic self-attackers who go the drug route damage themselves the most. They create a leak in their etheric body that takes a long time to heal—if they have not gone beyond the point of no return.

If you have a friend who is his or her own psychic attacker via drugs, you as a metaphysician can determine the fact without them knowing just what you are doing. Here is how:

Metaphysical Action Plan to Identify Drug Takers Through Radiesthesia

1. Have several people stand in a row including the person you suspect may be taking some hallucinogenic, hard drug, or even smoking pot excessively.

2. Stand behind them. Take a deep breath to relax. Starting at your left, hold your left hand over the head of the first person. Close your eyes.

3. Tell yourself that you feel energy discharge if it is leading out of the etheric body or psychic envelope. Tell yourself that you will feel it as a warmth on your palm or a tingle in your palm.

4. Move your left hand, palm down, in a sweeping motion around the top of the head of the first person, from ear to ear, staying about four inches above the hair.

5. Repeat for each person, noting any sensation in your palm. A psychic energy leak will be felt at some point at the side or top of the head. There will be no mistake about the difference in feeling at that point.

Slight feelings of psychic leakage indicate a healing possibility; strong tingling or heat feelings at one cranial point could indicate a person that has already done irreparable harm to himself with drugs.

There is little point in making metaphysical corrections in a person's etheric body if it is going to be punctured again by further drug usage. However, if such usage is discontinued, you can apply the methods of metaphysical correction described in Chapter 8,— "suturing" or "heat-sealing" the breaks.

If you are your own psychic attacker—light is your answer. Only the power of light can dispel the gloom. Light should be brought into your life in every possible way—physical and metaphysical.

Here are some of the physical ways:

- Eat out of white or brightly colored dishes.
- Be outdoors as much as possible on sunny days.
- Turn more lights on after dark.
- Wear white or brightly colored clothes.
- Switch to white night clothes and bedding.
- Keep all shades up, venetian blinds open, and curtains parted in office and home.
- Go without a hat.

Here are some metaphysical ways to bring light into your life:

- Associate with positive, enthusiastic people, avoiding negative pessimists.
- Emphasize fresh fruits and vegetables in the diet, switching from dense foods such as beef and pork.
- Get plenty of sleep, making sure that thoughts of serenity and assurance prevail at times of relaxation prior to sleep.
- Perform metaphysical action plans daily that surround you in brilliant white light, as described earlier.
- Help other people to become more positive.

How Sam T. Changed His Life Once He Discovered He Was His Own Psychic Attacker

Sam T. had been a successful metal sculptor. However, he got in with a pot-smoking crowd and gradually became immobilized. He could not get himself together to do anything except exist during the day. Then there were long pot sessions and his "chick" at night.

Sam and his friends stopped in one evening at a hall where the author conducted weekly training sessions in the development of ESP and metaphysical skills. Sam began smoking less, meditating more. He used Alpha Picturing to see himself sculpting once more. Within a few months, the group he was with split in two—those who preferred to stay with pot, and those who wished to find a more meaningful path. The latter group was led by Sam, who devoted himself more and more to helping others find themselves.

This group became a creative community for a while but then each individual went his own way. Sam's "chick" left him for a rock musician. Sam started distributing his metal sculptures in art galleries and gift stores and soon made a name—and a good living—for himself in this field.

Is Protection from Psychic Probing by Other Metaphysicians Possible?

In earlier chapters, I told you to penetrate walls to observe other people and how to "put on their heads" to know their thoughts and feelings.

Can you prevent this from happening to you?

This is a gray area in metaphysics. You can protect yourself from attack as already explained, but whether or not you can protect yourself from information-gathering sorties by other metaphysicians remains highly improbable.

There was, however, one instance where I was successful:

How I Blocked the Probing of Another Metaphysician

At a recent metaphysical conference, a panel of specialists skilled at reading other people were demonstrating their ability. The moderator called persons up from the audience to be "read." The "readers" were quite accurate. Then the moderator called me.

I was to be read by a young man. But I do not invite this sort of thing. I didn't ask for it then, and I would have refused but I did not want to throw a damper on things.

So I went up on the stage and as I stood by the young fellow I threw up a protective screen of love-light around me.

"You have a peaceful look," began the young man, "but behind that mask lies turmoil, both sexual and professional."

I knew immediately what had happened. So did the moderator. She handed me the microphone and suggested I read the young man.

"I believe that due to certain circumstances you have 'read' yourself, not me."

The moderator, an excellent psychic in her own right, nodded her head in assent. The young man just sat there. When I returned to my seat, a young lady came over to me. "I date him," she confided, "and you're perfectly right."

On the other hand the case of Mrs. Katherine L. was almost tragically unsuccessful. She had gone to the Soviet Union to visit her son. While there, she had a feeling she was being watched. Then something happened that really shocked her. She began to "hear" the Russians talking to each other and reporting on what she was saying to her son and even describing her thoughts.

Whatever method was being used, it misfired in some way, as Mrs. L. was not supposed to hear herself being "bugged." But she did. Even when she returned home, the "bugging" continued over thousands of miles. Only now, knowing she was "hearing" them, the treatment became oppressive rather than information-seeking.

It was then that Mrs. L. sought assistance from me, as well as several government agencies, and medical people. Interception or blocking efforts failed. The only relief that could be brought to this case was psychological instruction to Mrs. L. to effectively insulate herself from the psychic goings-on.

Perhaps one day, we will have effective protection against being psychically "bugged." Meanwhile, metaphysicians continue to "read" other people at will.

Seven Tips for Metaphysical Protection

There are no accidents in the world of metaphysics. Effect follows cause. If you are attacked psychically, you have invited it.

Take the Ouija board. Two people sit down opposite each other, and put their hands over a slider placed on a board with letters and numbers. They then ask for an answer to a question, or they may ask for a message to come through. Their hands begin to move and a message is spelled out, apparently by some influence or entity.

These Ouija board "players" invite trouble. They are issuing a blanket invitation to be "possessed."

"Come on in, anybody. Move my hands. My brain and nervous system are yours."

One woman fainted dead away several minutes after she started a Ouija board session with her sister. She had to be hospitalized for two days before she got her senses back from whoever had "moved in." There have been many similar cases in connection with Ouija boards.

Metaphysicians do not use the Ouija board (if they do, they know how to protect themselves), but they do expose themselves in other ways to possible psychic attack.

Here are seven ways to prevent your coming under psychic attack as a practicing metaphysician:

1. *Attune yourself to higher energies.* If you permit your mind to dwell on possession, black magic, evil witches, and other negativities, you are on their wavelength.

2. *Direct your metaphysical queries to a specific source.* When you ask to see the future, for instance, ask your Higher Self, or God, or some specific high entity. To "broadcast" queries invites "pranksters" to reply.

3. *Mind your own business.* Do not attempt to enter somebody's else's dispute, health problem, or other situation without being invited. Trespass invites trespass in return.

4. *Remain in possession of your senses.* Dulling the senses with alcohol, drugs or other materials creates the vacuum that psychic invaders watch for.

5. *Guard your health.* Proper nutrition, proper exercise, proper sleep keeps up your resistance—to metaphysical as well as physical invaders.

6. *Meditate regularly.* Daily Alpha Picturing of white light and attunement to the Highest creates protection.

7. *Think "protection."* Feel safe and you are safe. Fear attack and you open yourself to it!

11

Cosmic Metaphysics: Key to Locating Best Markets, Mineral Veins, Sunken Treasures, Lost Valuables

In an exclusive interview with the *National Enquirer* in February, 1974, Texas oil magnate John R. Shaw tells how he once tried to kill himself because he had lost his millions in part through unsuccessful oil drillings. Then, he said, he met psychic Ralph "Doc" Anderson who made him rich again by accurately pinpointing over 30 consecutive oil strikes.

The first "hit" came when Shaw and Anderson flew to Dallas and drove to a piece of land Shaw had never drilled because of a negative geologist report. There "Doc" Anderson began to walk around. Suddenly he walked more slowly. Then blood gushed from his hands without any visible cuts or openings. Shaw later drilled on that spot and quickly struck oil. It was his first strike in seventy tries over the previous four years. "Doc" Anderson then led him over the next few years to over thirty more successive strikes.

Every human being has the sensing devices to know the location of oil, water, and mineral resources. In some people, these sensing devices are not very well developed. In others, they are uncanny.

Some people need a tool such as a pendulum, divining rod, or dowsing stick. Other people use their own body as does "Doc" Anderson. Still others need no tool at all.

You have this ability to sense riches beyond your wildest dreams. In this chapter you learn how to put that ability to profitable use.

How to Penetrate the Cosmic Mind Where All Knowledge Lies

Take a look at your hand. Imagine you are one of its fingers. If you look at that finger, you see that it ends in a nail. Picture your conscious mind as being the length of the finger, while your subconscious mind is the fingernail.

This fingernail belongs exclusively to you. It is shared by no other finger. It contains all the information and experiences that you have acquired.

But where is your superconscious mind? Follow your finger in the opposite direction toward where it joins your palm. That is comparable to your superconscious. Note that it is shared by other fingers (people.) Note also that it is connected to the entire "body" of consciousness.

So, in a way, your conscious mind is "connected" to the entire body of consciousness. All you need to know is how to penetrate the veil that protects your conscious privacy by separating you from the all-knowing consciousness of which you are a part.

How Miss Naomi U. Found Lost Documents

In one of my University classes in ESP, a young woman, Miss Naomi U., asked if I could help her find some vitally important business papers. Since she had learned to go to her alpha level of mind, I asked her to do so and then to picture a clock with the hands at 2 p.m. and to accept the fact that the papers would be found at that time.

The next day she returned. "I must tell you all what happened," she said, addressing the class. "At 2:15 p.m. I suddenly realized I had been chatting with a neighbor for a half hour. I blew it, I thought. Then, I called my colleague at the office. 'Guess what?' my colleague said, 'I found the papers.' 'When?' I asked. 'Oh, about 15 minutes ago.' "

Was it Miss U's subconscious at work? Or her superconscious?

Obviously, since it involved another person's mind, a larger intelligence than the limited subconscious was involved.

There have been many similar cases where only the subconscious was involved. For instance, a young woman lost a check. She needed the money. She did not want to have to go through the long procedure of having the remitter stop payment and then send a duplicate. She went to her alpha level. I triggered her subconscious to reveal the whereabouts of the check by saying "At 10:30 this evening, you will know where the check is."

At 10:30 that evening, she suddenly thought of her husband's black leather jacket. She asked him where the jacket was. He replied in the trunk of the car. She looked and found the check in the jacket pocket.

On another occasion, a young man could not find his savings passbook. He needed money the next day. He, too, was practiced at relaxing to the alpha level. It was 8:30 p.m.; I instructed his subconscious. "At 9:30, you will know where the passbook is." He phoned later. "You were five minutes late. At 9:35, I felt the urge to look in a dresser drawer and found the passbook in a shirt pocket."

But getting back to Miss Naomi U., where the superconscious seemed to be working, too.

How did we manage to penetrate into this larger intelligence? There is nothing to it. It happens automatically.

You heard me right. It just happens.

If the subconscious is given an order that involves information not programmed into it, it forwards that order to the superconscious.

"This does not compute. Referred to Higher Authority."

You usually prevent this from happening, and that is the only real advantage that a metaphysician has. He knows how to get out of his own way. Everybody else *knows* that he is a separate intelligence, limited by past conditioning and learning.

Everybody, except the metaphysician, knows he cannot possibly come up with knowledge he never learned. That *knowing* that he can't makes it so.

The metaphysician *knows* he can. And that knowing makes it so.

Of course, there are a lot of stages in between—people who think it might be possible. For them, sometimes it happens, sometimes it doesn't.

You penetrate the Cosmic Mind by erasing the illusion of separateness from it, and *knowing* you are part of it and it is part of you.

If the Cosmic Mind could be said to have pulsations, they would in effect be at the alpha level. The reason this appears to be so is because the alpha level is the center of our mind's pulsations.

The average beta "high" is 21. If we center our conscious mind at the half-way point, this is 10½, or right in the middle of the alpha band (7 to 14).

Whenever you are at the center of something, you are able to encompass it better. So it is that by going to our alpha level we become more "connected," or in touch with, both the subconscious and super-conscious.

At the end of Chapter 4, you performed a metaphysical action plan to harness cosmic power so that it could operate in your life. Later, in Chapter 6, there was another metaphysical action plan utilizing the mantra "OM." If you would like to now reinforce your unity with Cosmic Mind, the following action plan uses both of these techniques to help you implement your universal "marriage."

Metaphysical Action Plan to "Marry" Your Consciousness with Cosmic Consciousness

1. Relax deeply.

2. Send your conscious soaring to embrace the blue sky as a lover. Soon you have within your consciousness the billions of suns within this galaxy.

3. Now move out further to instantly embrace millions of galaxies.

4. The universe is now all within your consciousness. Listen to it. It makes a sound like "OM."

5. Echo the sound of the universe by intoning "OM" three times. Understand it to mean the marriage vow, "I do."

6. Return your consciousness to this galaxy, this room. And end your session feeling married to a magnificent "mate."

Miracles You Can Now Perform with a Simple Pendulum

Even though your consciousness is "married" to Cosmic Consciousness, communications can still be a problem—as in any marriage.

Scientifically speaking, the energy transfer from Cosmic Consciousness to your superconscious may be adequate to create a perceptible signal, or thought, but the conductivity between your superconscious and your conscious may not be adequate to transmit that thought all the way. In other words, your superconscious may know, but you may not.

There is a method to increase the conductivity between your superconscious and conscious—to permit that perceptible signal from Cosmic Consciousness to go all the way. The method involves the use of a standard psychological tool called the pendulum. Psychologists use the pendulum to increase communication from the subconscious to the conscious. Metaphysicians use the pendulum to permit signals to pass from the superconscious to the conscious.

A pendulum is as simple a gadget as a button on a string. The button, metal washer, or other balanced object is tied to the end of a six-inch piece of thread or string. The loose end of the string is held above a table top so that the weighted end can swing freely.

How Shipwrecked People Were Located with a Pendulum After Planes Gave up the Search

A group of Australian sportsfishermen were cruising the New Hebrides area when a storm hit. Their wives called the authorities to report them missing. An air search was conducted among the myriad of islands that dot the area. After several fruitless days, the search was abandoned.

One of the wives heard about a local psychic. She went to see her. The psychic took out a map of the New Hebrides-Solomon Islands area. She laid it on a table and held a pendulum over it. She moved it slowly around the area the fishing party was known to have headed for, making larger and larger circles.

Suddenly the pendulum became agitated—that is, it began to swing. "Here," said the psychic, pointing to an obscure island. "They are here."

A boat was sent to that spot and found the shipwrecked party there, well, and happy to be rescued.

There is a simple method to start the pendulum working for you. It will take about five minutes. From then on, the pendulum will be your metaphysical communication link. It can be the most valuable investment of time you have ever made.

Metaphysical
Action
Plan to
Put the
Pendulum
to Work
for You

1. Sit comfortably at a table with your elbow positioned so that your forearm is nearly vertical and the pendulum held so that it just clears the table.

2. With the pendulum stationary, close your eyes; relax.

3. Visualize the pendulum swinging from left to right, right to left. Open your eyes and see if it is beginning to swing from side to side. Do this several times until you get a consistent and fairly good swing.

4. Do the same with a forward and back movement. Repeat until you get a consistent and pronounced swing (at least one-half inch amplitude.)

5. Now with your eyes open, ask, "Superconscious, am I ready to use the pendulum? If so, give me a sign." If there is involuntary movement of the pendulum, you are ready to use it. If not, repeat steps 1 through 5 until there is such a "sign."

Here is a way you can now test the pendulum to assure yourself that you are receiving trustworthy communication through it:

A. Draw a rough sketch of your house or apartment floor plan.

B. Think of an object that could be in one room or another. Be sure there is some legitimate doubt about its location.

C. Assume the pendulum position—forearm nearly vertical, wrist and fingers relaxed.

D. Move the stationary pendulum slowly around the floor plan until you get a sudden motion, no matter how slight.

E. Look in that part of the house to confirm the pendulum's communicative accuracy.

How to Determine if There Is Any Money Hidden in Your House or Buried Nearby

The pendulum's uses are infinite. Your ingenuity need only identify a need and the pendulum does the rest. However, it is best to start with simple tasks like finding lost objects at home or in the office and graduating to bigger and better prizes.

Remember, it is not your subconscious that is being tapped when you direct a question to your superconscious. So the knowledge you seek may very well be outside your own personal experience. For instance, suppose the family that lived in your house or apartment before you left, forgot they had secreted some money on the premises. With the pendulum, you can locate it, and claim it:

Metaphysical
Action
Plan to
Locate
Hidden
Money or
Valuables

1. Make a rough plan of your house, showing location of rooms, hallways, stairs, closets, etc. Make another rough plan of your grounds showing location of house, driveway, walks, and a major tree or two or other landmark.

2. Sit with the house plan on the table under your pendulum. Close your eyes, turn them upwards, and ask to be shown where any hidden money or valuables are located. Open your eyes.

3. Move the pendulum slowly over the plan in an orderly fashion, so as to blanket the entire plan, and maintain the pendulum arm stationary. Next, do the same with the grounds plan.

4. When there is a swinging movement of the pendulum, go over that area again to see if motion repeats. If so, create a detailed map of that spot and repeat procedure for a more exact location.

Warning: You can use this method to locate and appropriate valuables not on your property, belonging to somebody else, and it will work. But the superconscious that you use will not let it rest there. It will lead the injured party and/or authorities directly to you.

A young woman sewed several hundred dollar bills inside a dress. She returned home one day to find her phonograph and other valuables gone, including the secreted cash. A name kept popping into her mind over the next few days. It was a youth who had once told her how he could dowse for water. She had no reason to suspect this person, but nevertheless told police. They found her items in his garage and later retrieved part of the cash in return for a suspended sentence.

How to Probe Cosmic Consciousness
for Best Business Locations and Marketing Opportunities

Once you use the pendulum to assist you in tapping your superconscious on localized problems, like your home, you are ready to go on to bigger and better projects.

These usually involve maps rather than floor plans. In fact, the area may be so large that your superconscious automatically taps the Cosmic or Universal Mind for the answer.

Suppose you are starting a business. Where do you locate it? What state? What town? Even when you make these decisions you are still faced with the optimum street location, especially if it is a retail business.

Each year 400,000 small firms go out of business in the United States—100,000 in their first year. The Service Corps of Retired Executives (SCORE) who voluntarily assist small businessmen, report that a lack of proper business records is the prime reason, but next on the list is lack of business experience. This leads to poor location and similar inept judgments that spell inadequate sales volume.

SCORE supplies a valuable service here. In a way, it is the voice of a vaster experience to augment your own. But there is an even vaster experience. It is the sum total of all experience stored in the Universal Mind of which we are part.

You can use the pendulum to tap that Mind.

Let us assume you have decided to open a clothing store in your home town. Before you use the pendulum to determine a street location, you need to focus your idea of a clothing store more precisely. Men's or women's or both? High price, popular price, or discount price? Conservative or mod? These decisions affect the matter of location. Be prepared to have a detailed picture of your store before you begin this metaphysical plan.

Metaphysical
Action
Plan to
Determine
Best
Street
Location
for a
Retail
Store

1. Obtain a street map of town or city in which you wish to locate a retail outlet. Place it on a table and prepare to use your pendulum over it.

2. First, relax, close your eyes, and visualize the interior of the store or outlet. See the kind of merchandise or services you will offer. See customers buying. See them fitting the age, sex, and economic level the store will be catering to.

3. Remove the visual image, turn your eyes upward toward your superconscious and ask to be shown the best location for this store.

4. Open your eyes, and guide your pendulum over the street map until a movement occurs. Mark the spot.

5. Continue to blanket the street map, noting if a second or third movement occurs, again marking these spots.

6. End your session and visit all of the locations. Look around. Be able to picture the spot.

7. Return and do this follow-up test: Place the pendulum over each marked location. As you do, close your eyes and visualize it. Open your eyes and note the amplitude of the pendulum swing.

8. The largest amplitude of swing indicates the choice location.

Find Veins of Gold, Mineral Deposits and Buried Treasure

The scene is a vacant beach. The Sunday crowds have left. A lone figure is on the sand. He has a metal detecting device with which he "sweeps" the sand. It makes a clicking sound. Suddenly the clicking sound accelerates. He bends down, scoops up some sand in a sieve, picks a coin out of it, pockets it, and continues to sweep.

Another scene. It is also a sandy area but this time it is arid pastureland. Two men are moving about on it. One has a forked stick which he holds out in front of him. Suddenly the stick appears to move downward as the man struggles to keep it straight. "Here," he says. A well is dug. Water is found. And a year later the arid land has become verdant pasture.

A third scene. It is a hunter's lodge in the Rocky Mountains. A man is holding a pendulum over a topographical map. There is a movement of the pendulum. He marks the spot. Soon he has staked a claim and has made a valuable mineral "find."

Which scene do you choose?

I have talked to "electronic beachcombers." Some with sophisticated equipment average $50 a day in coins, rings, and other "finds." If your tried to locate these coins with a pendulum, you would be left far behind.

Dowsers are quite successful in locating water. You can miss an underground stream by just a few feet and wind up with a dry well, but the dowsing rod is precise. Given the choice of dowsing rod or pendulum looking for water, I would choose the dowsing rod, even though both act as a communicative link to the Cosmic Mind.

But take the dowser and the electronic beachcomber out to gold country, and you the metaphysician with a pendulum will mine circles around them. Scene number three is the one you want. It is the path to nature's riches.

Metaphysical Action Plan to Locate Gold, Silver, and Other Valuable Mineral Deposits	1. Obtain a relief map or topographical map, preferably covering no larger an area than a state. Prepare to use a pendulum over it.
	2. Relax, turn your eyes upward, and ask to be shown the location of gold deposits.
	3. Open your eyes. Move the pendulum over the map, noting spots that cause some agitation of the pendulum.
	4. Repeat step 2 for silver, copper, or other minerals which you must name specifically.

How Captain Alex J. Used the Pendulum to Find Evidence of the Lost Continent, Atlantis

Captain Alex J. was intrigued with the idea that evidence of the legendary sunken continent of Atlantis might be found through psychic or metaphysical means. He used the pendulum over a map of the Bimini-Florida area and found an area of pendulum agitation not too far off the coast of Florida. He went diving there and found strange masonry structures barely showing above the sand. He made a few dives with an underwater camera to capture his evidence photographically. Experts have not been able to give the photographs any explanation other than what they purport to be.

Miraculous Answers that the Pendulum Can Provide

When the pendulum was first used, it was found to be a valuable tool in communicating with the subconscious mind. It circumvented hours of psychiatric probing and hypnotic regression.

However, in order for it to work, you had first to establish a code or language for it to use. In addition to the visualizing step that we used to establish communications earlier in this chapter, a second step had to be successfully accomplished in which you had to ask which way was "yes" and which way was "no" until you received consistent responses from the pendulum.

Two more movements—clockwise and counterclockwise—permit two more responses: "I don't know" and "I won't tell." With

these responses set up by "agreement" with the pendulum, questions
are then asked relative to psychological causes that require a "yes" or
"no" answer. Gradually, an event can be identified by time, place, and
persons.

The metaphysician need not go through this procedure. Yet, he
can still get verbal answers from the pendulum over an even more
flexible range. Here is how:

A. Take a large sheet of paper or cardboard and divide each edge ten
times.

B. Write the letters of the alphabet around the edges and the numbers
one through 10. Since there are 37 squares this leaves one blank.
Draw in it the Om sign shown in the center of the wheel of Fortune
(Plate III) in Chapter 6.

C. In two corners, just inside the squares, write "yes" and "no." In the
other two corners write "perhaps" and "unlikely."

D. Now hold the pendulum in the center of the board. Close your eyes. See
the pendulum moving to a particular letter.

E. Open your eyes. Is it swinging toward the letter? Repeat until you get a
consistent response.

You are now ready to ask your superconscious almost any question and get a reasonably dependable answer. Most metaphysicians
find the pendulum to be 80 percent accurate.

It is not that your superconscious is inaccurate 20 percent of the
time. But the conscious mind is not sealed completely out of the
picture and can "interfere." What is really interfering is the intellectual or critical faculty of the conscious mind.

You can limit this interference by not trying to second guess the
pendulum. Do not entertain any preconceived ideas of the answer. For
instance . . .

You want to know where your girl-friend is tonight. You have a
strong suspicion she may be visiting Tom. You ask the pendulum. You
get a swing toward T, then O, then M.

This could be right or wrong. The strength of your conscious will
sends a much more powerful impulse to the muscles that operate the
pendulum than does the superconscious mind.

Another possible source of inaccuracy is the choice of which end
of the pendulum to record. However, since the common letters A
through P are opposite the less common letters Q through Z, and the

numerals, it is usually obvious which is being pointed to by the pendulum.

Here then is the procedure:

Metaphysical Action Plan to Obtain the Answers to "Impossible" Questions from the Pendulum

1. Ask the question while sitting relaxed, with the pendulum over the center of sheet, eyes closed and turned slightly upward. State mentally that you are directing the question to your superconscious.

2. Open your eyes and watch the pendulum "point" to letter after letter, recording these letters. Symbols and abbreviations are often used by the superconscious, which you need to then interpret.

Here are some of the types of questions you can ask the pendulum:

- Should I buy or sell _____?
- What is the best job for me?
- Where should I be living?
- When will I strike it rich?
- How will I strike it rich?
- Should I travel to _____ now or later?
- Where should I go on my vacation?
- Should I marry_____?
- How can I grow spiritually?

The pendulum's list is endless. Its metaphysical miracles are boundless.

You can be its beneficiary.

12

How to Use Your Metaphysical Power to Make the Right Decision Every Time

Many people who have studied metaphysics and started to use it successfully have changed their life style. Things seem to drop away from them that seemed quite important not too long before.

Some give up smoking. Some cut down on drinking to only an occasional glass of wine. Some no longer enjoy steak, roast beef, and hamburgers, and seem to lean more to fish and poultry. Some cut down on office time and try to spend more time out of doors. Some watch less television, spending that time in some other quiet way.

I'm not talking about three-pack-a-day smokers, potential alcoholics, or extremists in any of these matters. They probably would not have been attracted to metaphysics in the first place. It is the moderates that give way to change. Why?

I believe it is due to their increased attunement to the Universal or Cosmic Consciousness. They naturally want for themselves what nature wants for them.

Excessive drinking has always been known to be a risk. However, only in the past decade has smoking been officially recognized as "dangerous to health."

Now, the chemicals injected in beef are under increasing suspicion and the emissions of television tubes are being judged more soberly.

As to artificial light versus natural light, the recent findings are even more dramatic. Apparently, man needs the full spectrum of the sun's light in order to enjoy optimum efficiency of body and mind.

At a cancer research lab of the University of Chicago, it has been found that artificial light turned the hair of rats coarse and brittle and some turned completely bald. Rats exposed to pink light lost their tails, developed calcium deposits and had behavioral problems. On the other hand male rats exposed to full sunlight lost their tendency toward cannibalism and instead helped female rats care for the litter.

In his book *Health and Light*, Dr. John N. Ott, director of the Environmental Health and Light Research Institute in Sarasota, Florida, tells how researchers have discovered why chickens lay more eggs when ordinary incandescent lights burned into the night. It is not as one might conjecture—the chickens think it is still daylight and work that much longer. Actually the light affects the pineal and pituitary glands, triggering the increase in egg production.

When the late Dr. Albert Schweitzer's daughter returned from Africa, reporting the onset of cancer among African natives where none had been previously known to occur, Dr. Ott asked half-jokingly whether sunglasses had arrived there. She looked rather startled for indeed they had. Natives wore sunglasses as a sort of status symbol—some wearing nothing else.

Life needs natural light. Metaphysicians, attuned to the Cosmic Mind, are moved in the direction of their needs—physical and mental. By going to your alpha level and feeling a sense of belonging and cooperation with Cosmic Mind, you develop uncanny judgment and everything seems to go right for you.

Metaphysical Picturing that
Helps You Become a Business Genius

As a metaphysician, you now have a normal tendency to make the right business decisions. Some of these may appear to flout reason and contradict normal economic laws. Yet, when the dust has settled, they emerge as the right decisions.

This tendency toward "psyching in" on the right decision is enhanced by periods of quiet alpha level relaxation and by picturing light uniting your consciousness with a larger universal consciousness.

How Mr. Sanford W. Made a
Million in Spite of Himself

Mr. Sanford W. went through several business ventures and emerged with less than he went in with. Then he got into theater work. While directing and producing on Broadway, he met a spiritual leader in New York who inspired him to spend time each day relaxing and "feeling at one with the universe." Mr. W. began attracting the right manuscripts, skilled actors, and bigger audiences. Soon the money was rolling in.

He decided he needed sound investment opportunities. While at the alpha level, he felt moved to take a trip to Texas. There he invested in certain industrial property which doubled in value practically overnight. These fortuitous decisions occurred again and again. Today he is a millionaire, spending less time working at making money, more time at writing and speaking on the advantages of periods of relaxed oneness with the universe.

There are an infinite number of ways to erase the illusion of separateness and restore the reality of being a cell in the Universal Mind.

So far you have:

● Sent your consciousness out to embrace this galaxy and all others.

● Wooed the universe as a lover.

● Filled your consciousness with universal light.

● Intoned the universal mantra "OM."

● Felt a oneness with the universe.

● Tapped the Universal Mind through your superconscious mind.

For many, a universal concept is difficult to "feel." There needs to be a more graduated approach to the infinite ideal. So, some metaphysical methodology takes this into account by providing a few steps upward along the way.

You can devise these steps upward as well as anybody else. In fact, better. For instance, if a missionary attempts to provide a native with a step toward the concept of God by providing him first with the concept of Jesus, the native may be unable to do as well with that concept as he might do with the concept of smaller gods of the sea, of the wind, or of the mountain.

A man may have to go through a number of "step-up transformers" to eventually accept himself as part of something bigger than he is. It might go something like this:

- Member of the family
- Member of the firm
- Member of a political party
- Resident of a state
- Citizen of a nation
- Member of the human race
- Expression of life

You may prefer a spatial approach yourself where your universe is:

- Your room
- Your home
- Your home and school or office
- Your town
- The earth
- This planetary system
- This galaxy
- All space

Another method might be the religious approach. In Christianity, this might be:

- Local minister
- National religious leader
- International religious leader
- A saint
- Jesus

The successful metaphysician is constantly seeking to expand his consciousness in such ways—and to purify it by freeing it of negative concepts of limitation (*I can't*).

True, there are methods of acquiring specific information metaphysically, which help you to make correct decisions. But decision-making is often a continuous spur-of-the-moment process, one where

taking time out for Alpha Picturing through walls or putting on somebody else's head to tap their intentions can be a tedious matter.

We will review these latter procedures as a means to decision-
making, but your first priority for accurate decision-making should be
to remove the separations between you and the universe, and giving
your decision-making mind the benefit of Universal Mind. It is like
using a magnifying glass that enlarges a billion times.

Do a metaphysical action plan using your own "step-up transformers." I will merely call them numbers 1 through 10. Devise them
yourself along the lines of your own expansion of consciousness from
you to *universe*.

Metaphysical
Action
Plan for
Tapping the
Wisdom of
Universal
Mind
Permanently

1. Relax. Deepen your relaxation.

2. Be aware of yourself. Marvel at the working together
   of all of your living cells as one person. Love yourself.

3. Be aware of yourself in connection with #1 "step-up
   transformer." Feel love for #1. Feel the bond between you.

4. If you can be successful feeling oneness with #1,
   proceed to do likewise with #2, keeping #1 "in the
   picture." Feel love for #2. Feel love for #1. Feel,
   too, the love #1 and #2 have for each other and for
   you.

5. Continue to do likewise for additional "step-up transformers" until you feel you are stretched as far as you
   can go. End your session.

6. Repeat this metaphysical action plan a day or so later,
   moving from "step-up transformer" #1 to #2, etc.,
   and to the one you left off with plus at least one more.

7. Once you have united *you* with *universe*, you will
   likely have no need of the "step-up transformers"
   again. Take a moment to unite yourself with the universe daily.

How to Dissolve
Decision-Making Blocks

Impurities in metal increase its resistance to the flow of electrical
energy. Impurities in consciousness increase its resistance to the flow
of intelligence.

You can connect a motor to a source of power but if the connection is of a high resistance not enough power will get through it to run the motor.

Impurities of consciousness are acquired. The baby's consciousness begins to acquire impurities with the shock of being born. Then come insecurity, loneliness, fear—all brought on by threatening experiences.

I don't care who you are, what degrees you have, what corporate or political position you hold, how much money you have made, how popular you are—you have acquired impurities of consciousness. We all have these hang-ups, biases, fears or phobias, resentments, habits, and other aberrations from perfection.

If you recall, in the first few chapters, we attacked this problem in a general way. We used a kahuna technique for shaking negativity out of our body via our legs. Now we can focus on some specific impurity, one at a time, and eliminate each by another technique: Relive and Relieve.

Before you begin this metaphysical action plan, identify some problem, physical or psychological, which you would like to dissolve. If there are a few, place them in the order of priority that you would like to see them exit.

How Miss Caroline M. Got Rid of a Craving for Sweets She Had When She Had to Make Decisions

Miss Caroline M. became quite expert at Alpha Picturing and directing events in her life. She was a confident and effective person. However, she had a weakness for chocolate and other sweets that she could not control. She knew it was not good for health and the extra pounds it put on her lessened her confidence in herself as an attractive woman. But more important, she found that she would procrastinate about making decisions and instead hit the chocolates. She resolved it was an impurity of consciousness that was interfering with her perfection as a metaphysician and one that she would have to eliminate in order to progress further.

She relaxed and told her subconscious that she would like to know the major cause of this weakness for sweets. She then sat quietly, permitting her thoughts to reminisce. She found herself thinking about kindergarten—how the teacher taught them to cut out figures and paste them up. She tasted the paste. My, it was good. She kept tasting the paste. Occasionally, the teacher would catch her and reprimand her.

But she continued to sneak these tastes of the paste instead of deciding where to paste what.

When she ended her relaxation and reminiscing session she wondered about the connection between the paste in kindergarten and the sweet tooth today. If there was a connection, what a silly reason to be bugged by such a health sapper. She did not have to wonder very long. Apparently, just the reliving of this incident was enough to release her from her ties to sugar. As she put it, "I'm free at last!" She was able to make decisions without sorties to the candy box.

If you have a personality quirk, hang-up, bias, or physical problem identified, you are ready to perform this conscious purifying metaphysical process.

Metaphysical Action Plan to Dissolve Decision-Making Blocks and Help Purify Consciousness

1. Relax deeply.

2. State the problem to yourself.

3. State mentally to your subconscious mind, "I would now like to know the major cause of this problem."

4. Permit your mind to drift in a daydreaming, reminiscing way. If an experience comes to mind that seems pertinent, permit it to play itself out.

5. End your relaxation and review intellectually the experiences you have just relived. Can you see the causative connection with the problem? Does it seem stupid, ridiculous, perhaps ludicrous that such a cause with irrelevance today could have such an effect on you today?

6. This re-evaluation of the cause should dissolve it and the problem should begin to disappear.

7. Repeat this procedure on similar problems in the days ahead to continue the consciousness purification procedure.

Business executives keep a wary eye out for people in their organization with personal problems. They know that marital discord, drinking, or special eccentricities can interfere with the decision-making process. Business success requires "clear thinking."

Metaphysical success also requires "clear thinking." But its requirements go even further—toward purification of consciousness.

That is why some of the very first metaphysical work in this book was directed toward positive thinking.

It is a never-ending process. You need to be constantly aware of your own consciousness. This is a private matter between you and yourself. It should not be discussed with others.

When you discuss a matter such as this with others you do two things:

1. You discharge the energy of purpose that moves you forward.

2. You inadvertently acquire their secret opposition.

An artist who talks about the painting he will paint, may never get to paint it. The writer who talks about the book he will write, may never get to write it. Vocalizing shortcircuits the spark of volition.

Also, people inwardly resent your purifying your consciousness. Quietly they "crucify" you.

The purification of consciousness is the one occult metaphysical action which must remain secret. This is not because the methodology is to be known only by a few. That kind of occultism is out in this new age. It is because the knowledge by others of your doing so will negate your results. With a pure consciousness the Universal Mind and you work together, making all things possible.

So think pure, be pure, do pure.

Secretly.

Obtain Signals from Your Body as to Which Course to Take

The pendulum principle discussed in the previous chapter has an interesting decision-making application which you should know about.

He is selling. You are buying. You are far apart but negotiations have brought you closer together. Will he drop his price more? Or should you make the deal now?

You cannot say, "Just a moment while I play with this button or string." But you can do something else just as good without being observed.

The body is a pendulum. It can sway back and forth, or lean to the left or right. This leaning can be made to be a superconscious link to your conscious mind just as is the pendulum. Here is how:

Metaphysical
Action
Plan (A)
Get
Instant
Answers
from Your
Body

1. Relax in a standing position.

2. Close eyes and turn eyes upward.

3. Repeat the word "yes" mentally and lean to the right. Repeat the word "no" and lean to the left.

4. Now repeat the word "yes" mentally and visualize yourself leaning to the right. Repeat the word "no" mentally and visualize yourself leaning to the left. Do not move by conscious effort.

5. Open your eyes and repeat the word "yes" mentally followed by the command, "Lean!" and see if there is a slight leaning to the right. Repeat the word "no" mentally followed by the command, "Lean!" and see if there is a slight leaning to the left. Repeat steps 1 to 4 until step 5 shows consistent results.

6. Test yourself on valid but not critical problems. State the problem, followed by the command "Lean!" Get the answer "yes" or "no." Carry it out and determine if judgment is accurate. If this happens consistently you are ready to use this method on difficult or critical problems.

The pendulum method is generally accurate and trustworthy. One possible interference can come from conscious intellectualizing or prejudging. You can want the answer to be "yes," so you create a voluntary energy signal. You can consciously control this conscious interference by turning your thoughts upward (as you previously did with your eyes) at the moment of stating the command, "Lean!"

Leaning is just one way of getting a body response. Some metaphysicians prefer responses which do not require a standing position.

Here are other responses that can be induced:

● Tingling sensation in the shoulders.
● Tingling sensation in the hands.
● Movement of the forefingers.
● Heat sensation in the knees.

If you wish to augment your ability to receive metaphysical answers through your body, then select one of these body responses and do the metaphysical action plan (B).

Metaphysical Action Plan (B) Get Instant Answers from Your Body

1. Relax in a seated position, close eyes and turn them upward.
2. Repeat the word "yes" mentally and ask for the body sensation you selected to occur on the right side. Repeat the word "no" mentally and ask for that body sensation to occur on the left side.
3. Open your eyes and proceed as in Step 5(A), commanding the body sensation to occur.
4. Test as in step 6 (A).

Special Note: It is common for "yes" to be to the right, "no" to the left. If any inaccuracy occurs, proceed over again with Plans A and B, asking which side is "yes" and which side is "no." This could be especially applicable to left-handed people.

You can permit your body to use its own sensation as a signal as follows:

Metaphysical Action Plan (C) Get Instant Answers from Your Body

1. Relax in a seated position and turn eyes upward.
2. Repeat the word "yes" mentally and ask for a body signal. When you think you have received such a signal, repeat the word "no" mentally and see if you receive the same type of response either on the other side of the body or in some other way.
3. Proceed as in 5A and 6A using this response.

How Colonel Bert A. Received a Signal When He Met the Right Person

Bert A. was a retired colonel who had a great interest in metaphysical work. He "taught" his body to provide a signal in the form of a tingle in his shoulder to indicate whether a person he was dealing with was honest and sincere—a tingle in his right shoulder meant all was well, a tingle in his left shoulder was a danger signal.

These signals stood him in good stead when he received invitations to speak. He would hold the invitation and ask for a signal. Invariably, the body signals foretold correctly—either the success of meetings he attended, or the failure of those where he heeded his body's warning not to attend.

Colonel A. was able to develop these signals so that he could be "told" when he was talking to somebody whom he had known in a previous life. Hypnotic regression would confirm this, but Colonel A. could also use metaphysical means to go back in time to review the relationship.

How Dr. Dorothy P. Detected the Color of Auras by Her Own Body Signal

Dr. Dorothy P., a psychologist who taught metaphysics, could not see auras even though she taught others how to develop this ability. To compensate for this lack, she trained her body to provide a tingle on her left shoulder for the red side of the spectrum; on the right shoulder for the blue side of the spectrum; and various points on the back of the neck for colors in between.

This worked quite dependably for her, being confirmed visually by others. It not only helped her in her teaching of aura viewing, but now she could "see" the color of the aura of the person she was dealing with—thus becoming aware of the sincere or devious person.

Before we leave the subject of using the body as a pendulum, let me remind you that if the decision-making occasion permits you to retire to privacy where you can use your button on a string pendulum, the metaphysical methods provided you in the previous chapter are certainly applicable.

In the case of complicated questions, it is best to divide them up into simple components. For instance, your lawyer has made shocking fee demands before the trial despite a previously consented to fee arrangement. Do you negotiate? Do you appeal to the court to help? Do you dismiss him and take a new attorney, or some combination of these alternatives?

The order of your questions might be:

Question	Possible Reply
What do I do first to solve this problem?	Court
If the court goes against him, should I seek another attorney?	Yes
Whom?	Davies

These answers may lead to further questions which should also be simplified for best results.

The superconscious knows.

And it *is* telling.

How to Order a Dream
That Solves a Special Problem for You

The subconscious and superconscious talk to us nightly in dreams.

Dreams sponsored by the subconscious mind are attempts to get across psychological information that would help our conscious mind to know. Dreams sponsored by the superconscious mind are attempts to get across psychological information that it would help our conscious mind to know. Dreams sponsored by the superconscious mind are attempts to get across psychic information, happenings at a distance in time or space.

So you find that some dreams reveal you to yourself and some dreams reveal the future.

I am not going to cover dream interpretation. Not only is this a large field covered adequately by other books, but it is my personal opinion that nobody else can help you understand your dreams. You are your own best dream interpreter. Symbols used by dreams need to be examined by you for meaning personal to you. However, I am going to tell you how to control your dreams so that you can use them to your metaphysical advantage to get answers to problems.

How Mrs. Ruth J. Saved Her Job by Requesting an Answer in a Dream

Mrs. Ruth J. was a widow who worked for a large East coast department store. She was in the job only six months when her mother on the West coast was taken seriously ill. Since Thanksgiving was approaching along with the peak of holiday business, she was told that she could not take a leave of absence without forfeiting her job. Yet reports from West coast relatives indicated the end might be near for her mother.

Mrs. Ruth J. would gladly give up her job to be at her mother's side if indeed her death was imminent, but not for just another bedside visit. She decided to use a dream ordering technique. She relaxed deeply just before retiring and repeated mentally, "I want to have a dream explaining my mother's illness. I want to remember it and understand it."

Mrs. Ruth J. woke up in the early morning hours. She had seen her mother in a dream. She looked ten years younger. She was working in the kitchen and seemed to want to be left alone. She ordered her daughter to leave the kitchen. Then she woke up.

The message was clear. Mrs. Ruth J. decided to remain at work. She phoned the West coast every few days. Within a week, her mother was out of danger and convalescing.

Ordering a dream is even more simple than ordering a spare part—no special code number, no long wait for delivery. All you do is exactly what Mrs. Ruth J. did:

Metaphysical Action Plan to Get a Specific Answer in a Dream	1. Relax to your alpha level in bed, preparatory to falling asleep.
	2. Tell yourself mentally, "I want to have a dream to give me the answer to (state problem). I want to remember the dream and I want to understand it.
	3. When you awake, remember the dream. Understand its meaning as an answer to the stated problem.

The Decision About Which Decision-Making Technique to Use

You now have a choice of methods that permit your conscious problem-solving intellect to be reinforced by the sum total of all your experiences and learning via the subconscious, and by the sum total of universal wisdom via the superconscious.

The problem arises: Which problem-solving technique do you use?

To help you make such a decision, here is a round-up of these techniques and their areas of preferential use:

Travel Through Walls to Observe (Chapter 3)

Best where problems involve identities of friend and foe, and where general activities in progress affect decision.

Putting on Another Person's Head (Chapter 8)

Best where problems involve the thoughts, attitudes or intentions of one or more persons.

Alpha Relaxation and Picturing (Chapter 12)

Best where general goals and directives need to be determined. Works best after special metaphysical action plan to unite you with the universe, and the dissolving of major decision-making blocks.

Pendulum and Alphabet (Chapter 11)

Best for determination of specifics of an immediate solution, especially where "yes" and "no" answers do not suffice.

Body Signals (Chapter 12)

Spur of the moment decisions where pendulum cannot be applied, and where "yes" and "no" answers are all that are needed.

The decision is yours.

13

Miracle Metaphysics for Influencing the Weather, Natural Phenomena, and World Events

The energy of weather—wind, temperature, and their related meteorological activities—responds to the energy of consciousness. The American Indians knew this, and their rain chants still work today. The Hawaiians knew this and they have an effective rain chant, too, although theirs is used in reverse—to stop rain.

A group of people who work with me to solve human problems joined recently in an Alpha Picturing session to stave off a storm that was headed for Honolulu. The storm appeared to jump right over the city and hit the neighboring city of Kaneohe where it ripped off roofs and caused heavy flooding.

Flushed with this success, the next time we met at my apartment, three members had special weather needs they asked the group to help with: A teacher was taking her class to the other side of the island to study marine life on Friday, which was the next day. She wanted good weather from 10 a.m. on. A man was going on an all day hike Saturday. And a woman's daughter was getting married near Diamond Head on Sunday at noon. We put all three events on our "mental screen."

The next morning, Friday, was almost as dark as night. Lightning flashed continuously. At 10 a.m. sharp, my building was struck by lightning and the lights went out.

How could any metaphysician, tuned into the Universal Mind, not get such a clear message? I said to myself—no more interfering with the weather unless it's of monumental importance.

When the teacher returned, she phoned me to say the weather on the other side of the island was not bad, just a drizzle. The Saturday hiker had a beautiful day. And the Sunday wedding was held under blue skies.

Nevertheless, I now refrain from using my energy of consciousness to make meteorological changes unless the need is critical. How are you to determine if the need is critical? The method is built in to the next metaphysical action plan.

How to Melt a Cloud
with the Energy of Your Consciousness

This critical need to change the weather may come for you and you should know how to use your power of metaphysics to affect the weather should you have to. There is a simple method to prove to yourself that the energy of consciousness is real energy indeed and that it dwarfs physical energy in certain ways.

This metaphysical action plan is to demonstrate your powers to yourself. It is not advisable to "show off" to others that you can melt a cloud. In fact no matter how often you do it, they will not accept it as valid. They will attribute it to some trick—thinking, possibly, that you know something about the anatomy or behavior of clouds that they do not know. So, the following procedure is for your own private use.

Metaphysical Action Plan to Melt a Cloud

1. Pick a day when the sky is clear, but fluffy white clouds (cumulus) abound.

2. Standing where you can get a wide view of the sky, pick a control cloud and another cloud you will work on. Start with small clouds at first. If this is not possible, use the edge of two clouds, one as control, one to work on.

3. Gaze intently at the edge of the cloud you will melt, imagining that the cloud is only five feet above your head.

4. Bring the cloud down to a foot away. See the edge of it dissolving into thin vapory wisps, then nothing.

5. Compare with control cloud.

A Canadian man made quite a stir when he discovered he could melt clouds. He invited the press to watch as he did it and proved time and time again that he had the ability. Pictures of a cloud dissolving while the control cloud remained intact appeared in the newspapers and later in a book he wrote.

What his onlookers did not know was that they could do it, too. In fact, as they observed with expectation and belief, they were indeed helping him to do it.

Turning On Rain and Turning It Off

American Indians are known for their ability to live harmoniously with nature. For them it is not a case of man against nature that has contributed to the separations of most Western people, but man working with nature that contributes toward a feeling of belonging to the whole.

This oneness unites the consciousness with the superconsciousness, as we have found out, and enables the ordinary man to "will" extraordinary things.

So it was that the Indians were able to develop a chant that brought rain when it was needed. The rain chant became an oddity of our time. But the rain chant is only one way that the Indians cause it to rain. They have others. The Hopi, much of whose land does not lie along running water, pray for rain. After they pray it rains. Other tribes whose land does not lie along running water and who do not have to depend on prayer, have no belief in this method. And for them such prayers do not work.

How Mr. David Mililani Bray Stopped the Rain So the Show Could Go On

A pageant was scheduled for a special garden spot in Honolulu. Mr. David Mililani Bray, whose father was a well known kahuna (Hawaiian metaphysician), was on hand to give the opening chant. However, as the crowd gathered, so did the rain clouds. A light drizzle at show time, getting heavier by the minute, threatened to cancel the pageant.

I looked questioningly at David. He looked questioningly at the sky. Then he put on his ceremonial feathered cape and proceeded to render an unscheduled chant. Immediately the light rain stopped, and the sky brightened. The show went on. Forty-five minutes later, as the finale ended, the skies darkened and it poured for several hours.

What really happens when an Iroquois chant brings rain, a Hopi prayer causes showers, or a kahuna chant stops a downpour? The key word is "agreement." As part of the Universal Consciousness, your superconscious mind is involved in what is going on. That involvement may be only very slight. It could be as if you are part of a raceway crowd rooting for the favorite horse to hang on to his lead in the stretch.

But there is an involvement. You do have a voice in the weather. To make that voice heard, you need to speak on a universal level. Even then you need to evoke agreement—agreement by the Universal Consciousness, or the part thereof that is in control.

So there are two steps:

1. You go to your alpha level, attune yourself to your superconscious, and then *a step higher*.
2. You appeal to Universal Consciousness, working through its *appointed parts*, to change the condition.

"A step higher" and "appointed parts" are new concepts to you. Let me explain.

When you turn your eyes upward to a point above your head, you automatically attune, or address, yourself to your superconscious. You do not want to bypass your superconscious but you do want to bring it with you as you move your consciousness on to even "higher ground."

"Higher ground" need be only a few feet higher. A point above your head, a few feet higher—these are only semantic tools that consciousness responds to. Actually, the physical distances mean very little. In the metaphysical realms, up and down have no physical reality. Metaphysically, up means better (more of good) and down means worse (less of good.) Good is higher energy. So, *a step higher* to higher ground means higher energy. *Appointed parts* refers to that aspect of higher energy which is involved in weather control.

If you want a job with a certain large firm, you don't go to the president, you go to the personnel officer. It does not matter if his name is Smith or Jones, you get to the right "energy" by his title, *Personnel Officer*.

Similarly, if you want a job done regarding the weather, you need not know the name of the energy to whom Universal Consciousness assigns this responsibility—all you need to do is direct your request to "Rain Maker," "Cloud Former," or some equivalent terminology that fits.

Metaphysical
Action
Plan for
Turning
on Rain

1. Relax. Turn your eyes upward and then focus at a point ten to twenty feet above your head.

2. Consider the universal "Rain Maker" at that point. Call to "Rain Maker" mentally. Recite mentally the need for rain. Be eloquent in making a "case" for rain.

3. Slowly visualize clouds forming, evaluating how you feel. If there is a "heavy" feeling or unpleasant feeling, stop and continue Step 2. If three such attempts do not result in a pleasant, even joyous feeling, omit the visualizing procedure and end your action. On the other hand, once a joyous feeling accompanies the rain image, pursue it for several minutes before terminating the action.

I told you earlier that a built-in safety factor would be contained in your metaphysical action plan for rain-making. Of course, you see now that it is the way you feel while using your Alpha Picturing to bring about the result.

We did not observe this ourselves the evening before lightning gave us a message. But we use it now and no untoward events have occurred when weather changes were metaphysically effected.

How I Broke Up a Cloud
Bank in Ten Minutes

I and some friends had driven one hundred miles and traversed a narrow road that climbed some 7,000 feet to where the mountain dropped sheerly to the sea. As we approached the end of the road to reap the rewards of a notoriously breathtaking view, we saw that a cloud lay ahead. Sure enough, all there was to see was white cloud as far down as the eye could see. I told my friends to go back to the car for a few minutes. I did my Alpha Picturing with a special appeal to the "God of the Mountain." All we need is five minutes, I stated mentally. I received a good feeling so I began to dissolve the cloud bank. The rapidity with which that thick cloud began to dissipate surprised even me. I hurried back to the car to get my friends. By the time we returned, there was the sunlit view of the cliffs and ocean thousands of feet below. As we turned to go back to the car, clouds began to form again.

Why Weather Chants and Prayers
Seldom Work for the Non-Metaphysician

This control of the weather, and even of other more worldwide events, is the most incredible aspect of metaphysics to the initiate. How can one small person exert an influence over, say, a storm?

There is hardly a person alive who at some time in his or her life, even if only as a small child, did not pray for the wind, thunder, or rain to stop. And it kept right on blowing, thundering, or raining.

When man first chemically seeded the clouds by plane and caused it to rain, it was a dramatic breakthrough. Man was big enough to tackle natural phenomena.

Too small. Not big enough. These are terms that are meaningless in metaphysics. The metaphysician has worked on his consciousness to "marry" it to Universal Consciousness. His consciousness and the Universal Consciousness are united. All he needs to get is "agreement."

With this agreement, your consciousness is making the storm. You become part of the cause behind the effect. So, you can change the effect—alter the course or intensity of the storm. By contacting the appointed part, that is, the special part of Universal Consciousness that storm energy derives from, and making your plea or stating your case, you are applying for that agreement.

Contacting the appointed part is automatic. It is like moving your arm. You don't have to know the anatomy of the brain to do that. You just get the idea of "arm" and away you go. Likewise, you just get the idea of stormmaker and you are in touch.

The next step of making your case needs logic and reasonableness. But it also needs fervor. Your emotion is the voltage that causes energy of consciousness to flow.

The non-metaphysician feels out of it. So he is. He feels too small. So he is. He feels separated from the whole process. So he is. And furthermore, he sends his message into the air, falling on "ears" he knows not where. So it does.

How to Issue
Powerful Commands to Natural Forces

As a metaphysician, your switch is closed and you are connected. There is no resistance to the message as you *know* from experience you are getting through. You "dial" the correct party and you speak fervently enough to be heard.

In effect, *you are issuing powerful commands to natural forces.*

I say "in effect," because the idea of agreement is not compatible with the idea of command. You might say that, after obtaining agreement, you issue powerful confirmation.

Hurricanes, tornadoes, and other violent storms contain tremendous amounts of physical energy. Hurricanes can sweep paths of destruction scores of miles wide and hundreds of miles long.

When concentrated in tornado form, this energy can send trucks hurtling through the air and bring down sturdy buildings as if they were match sticks. Yet, hurricanes halt their forward progress, switch direction, peter out into tropical storm status, and then quit altogether. It is as if some mightier energy is at work.

Tornadoes form and then unform just as quickly. They descend and lift. They tighten and loosen. They, too, seem to be manipulated.

Man-ipulated might be the way to spell it. Man's consciousness invites storms and natural phenomena. It is not the only factor at work, but there are no accidents in the Universal Consciousness that controls all energy. Effect follows cause.

It is next to impossible for us, even as metaphysicians, to understand the reasons or causes behind certain devastating natural effects. They seem so arbitrary. Yet, you have a responsibility as a metaphysician to accept the wisdom of Universal Consciousness. You need to give your agreement.

If, on occasion, you wish to get agreement from the "Storm-Maker" of Universal Consciousness, then you have to give your understanding and agreement, too. You need to accept the validity and justice behind storm violence.

In India, the god Siva is the "Storm-Maker." Siva is the god of destruction but is accepted as a key energy in creation. Destruction is understood in India to be part of a never-ending cycle of creation, preservation, and destruction.

Yet, the time comes when a storm approaches and you are aware of important reasons why its destructive energy needs at this time to be averted.

You must, of course, vote no. And your vote can have the effect of a veto.

Metaphysical Action Plan to Bar the Approach of a Violent Storm

1. Relax. Turn your eyes upward to a point ten to twenty feet above your head.
2. Call to "Storm-Maker" mentally. Make your case fervently.
3. Visualize the storm missing your area. Test your feelings to see if you have agreement. If not, repeat Step 2. If so, continue this visualizing process for a few minutes.
4. End your Alpha Picturing, knowing the storm has been barred.

Your metaphysical action plan can be directed at:

- Storm-Maker
- Earthquake-Maker
- Flood-Maker
- Plague-Maker
- Pestilence-Maker
- Volcano-Maker
- Tidal Wave-Maker
- War-Maker

Your action is the same—directing your communication to the appropriate part of Universal Consciousness, getting agreement, and visualizing the solution.

How We Ended a Plague of Blackbirds in Maryland

A Maryland farm town woke up one morning to find the air black with birds—literally black—as the birds were crows, grackle, and other species of black birds. There were millions. They stayed in the area day after day, stripping the farms of everything growing and green. Nothing helped. Even shooting off cannons and shotguns only caused a temporary flurry among the birds who then settled back to their devastation.

I read about this phenomenon in the newspapers some 5,000 miles away. I asked fellow metaphysicians if they thought it was a project that invited our effort. They agreed. After all, two weeks of such a pestilence must have certainly accomplished whatever its initial purpose was. That night, our appeal at our alpha level was, "Enough!"

The next day, the paper carried the story that the birds had left. It was attributed to more shotgun blasts. They had left at dawn. Accounting for the time difference, the birds had departed three hours after our metaphysical commands. Coincidence? We know differently.

How Nature "Talks" to the Metaphysician Through Signs and Omens

Recently experiments were conducted by the Ernest Holmes Research Foundation and reported on in the July, 1974, issue of *Science of Mind*, concerning the effects of the energy of consciousness on a cloud chamber.

A cloud chamber is a device originally developed by nuclear physicists to make the path of nuclear particles visible. Dr. Robert N. Miller, Dr. Philip B. Reinhart, and Anita Kern used the cloud chamber in conjunction with Olga Worrall, internationally known psychic healer.

Olga Worrall concentrated her conscious energy on the cloud chamber and produced visible effects. She then traveled six hundred miles away and at an appointed time again concentrated her conscious energy on the cloud chamber. The distance meant nothing. Again, the same visible effects were produced by her conscious imaging.

Scientists seem to go through three stages in their acceptance of metaphysical phenomena: "You're crazy," "It's impossible," "We've known it all along." I for one do not begrudge the latter omniscient attitude as long as progress is made by science in investigating what have been "taboo" areas.

As this progress is made the map of consciousness will gradually be completed. We will understand the god-like powers of man's individual consciousness properly directed, and the existence of Universal Consciousness of which his is part. It will come none too soon, as man's feeling of separateness has been pitting him against nature rather than cooperating with nature to the extent that severe imbalances are occurring that threaten survival on the planet.

Some scientists, especially those working with metaphysical phenomena, are suspecting more and more that there is some force prevalent in the universe which has as one of its characteristics, intelligence, and that it is this intelligent force that supplies answers to the pendulum user or the dowser or the psychic. One scientist was recently quoted as believing that this force operates through the whole spectrum of energies and frequencies, hinting that it is omnipresent and omniscient.

Can this be what metaphysicians have been calling the superconsciousness?

A unified field of intelligence permeating the universe certainly answers a lot of questions. It brings science and religion a giant stride closer. And it helps to explain the theory of sychronicity, which states that everything that happens at one instant of time is related to everything else that happens at that instant.

The metaphysician is aware of this. He sees signs and omens around him constantly.

How Mr. Samuel R. May Have Been Saved from a Train Wreck by Birds

Mr. Samuel R. was driving along a country road at a good clip, when suddenly three birds flew across the path of the car from right to left, so close to the windshield that he instinctively ducked. Aware of his oneness with nature, Mr. R. felt there was a good chance the birds were telling him something.

He slowed up and as he rounded a bend he saw railroad tracks about one hundred feet ahead. He decided to slow down even more and just then a freight train roared through the intersection. It was going from right to left.

Birds are known to stop singing minutes before an earthquake. Dogs often howl when a person is dying. Nature speaks in many "voices."

Many primitive cultures contain similar portents or omens. A pregnant woman favors her right arm or leg. She will have a boy. A rainbow is seen. It signals approval.

The way nature communicates can be through the behavior of animals, the behavior of weather (mists, cloud formations, chill winds, whirlwinds,) and the behavior of other people, especially strangers

How these signs are interpreted is largely up to the observer.

Nature has no secret code. That would be defeating the purpose. Things happen which trigger reactions in you.

You can improve your own awareness through simple auto-suggestion:

Metaphysical   1. Relax.
Action Plan
to Increase   2. State mentally, "Each day I become more and more
Awareness of   aware of the sight, scents, and sounds around me that
Portents and   are meaningful to me. I sense portents, omens, and
Omens and   the communications to me by Universal Conscious-
Understand   ness and I understand them."
their Message   3. End relaxation. Repeat daily.

Once your awareness of signs and omens increases, nature or Universal Consciousness seems to use this channel of communication more frequently. This may just seem to be because of your increased awareness. But remember we are dealing with Intelligence. It is only natural and intelligent that once a line of communication is opened, it is more frequently used.

Metaphysical "Happenings" That You May Be Part of or Witness

As your consciousness opens itself to Universal Consciousness all things become possible.

This joining of your consciousness with the source of consciousness is known in India as yoga, meaning yoke or joining. Yogis use many techniques to accelerate this uniting of consciousness. The most popular, at least in the Western world, is hatha yoga. This is a form of quiet positioning of the body into pretzel-like shapes which, besides bringing better physical fitness, also seems to lead to a release of tension and greater peace of mind.

Other types of yogic disciplines include controlled breathing, controlled behavior, and controlled thinking with mantras, prayer, meditation, and creative visualizing all involved.

Breathing techniques are one of the most powerful yogic methods to join you with Universal Consciousness. I will provide you with a method of yogic breathing as a metaphysical action plan, but first a suggestion: Delay the use of this breathing technique until you have been a practicing metaphysician for a few months. You may decide to wait even longer as you find yourself already part of universal "happenings" that are dramatic and often astounding. The best way to describe this is that you begin to know things that you have no way of knowing, such as:

- You know that somebody will call or write just before they do.
- You know the moment somebody arrives back from the office, market, or errand.
- You know about a change in the weather before it happens.
- You know you should sell or buy.
- You know that you should go somewhere, or should not go.

Australian aborigines, who must develop their cooperation with nature for survival reasons, are known for their ability to go forth to greet visitors long before they could possibly know of their impending arrival. They seem to know details of the visit, such as the purpose and that two more members of the party will follow three days later.

Certainly, breathing techniques to enhance their connection with Universal Consciousness would be less necessary for these natives than for the Western metaphysician not as close to nature.

How Madame Farida Foretold the Appearance of Flying Saucers

A noted Indonesian sensitive was visiting in Japan and was being interviewed on television. Her ability to tune in on people using the lines on their palms to trigger her psychic powers was well known to me, to her wide circle of international admirers, and to the television reporter who was interviewing her. She "read" him through his hand quite impressively. However, he suddenly took a different tack. "Predict something, Farida," he suggested. She hardly paused.

"Next week, flying saucers will appear over Hokkaido."

Later, she worried, "How could I have been so bold to predict such a thing. Suppose it does not happen? What about my reputation?"

Next week, she was taken to Hokkaido by the news media. Television cameras and reporters were everywhere, gazing upward.

Then, suddenly, there they were. Three, then four, then five, flying in formation, then separately. Their appearance made the front pages. Farida was an overnight celebrity.

Certainly Madame Farida need not use the yogic breathing technique to tighten her closeness with Universal Consciousness.

Here is the yogic breathing technique for later use by you, should you deem it necessary to better integrate your consciousness with Universal Consciousness—and make things "happen." Often, what happens, happens immediately and can be in the form of a philosophical lesson or psychic prophecy.

Metaphysical Action Plan to Use Your Breath to Enhance Psychic Powers and Induce a Vision

1. Relax. Place hand on nose in such a way that you can alternately block first one nostril then the other with your fingers.

2. Inhale through the left nostril, blocking the right, slowly, to the count of 10. Hold breath to the count of 10 by blocking both nostrils. Breathe out slowly through the right nostril to the count of 10, by blocking the left nostril.

3. Reverse the process now, inhaling through the right nostril, holding, and exhaling through the left.

4. Repeat the full cycle for a total of three times.

5. Immediately on completion, permit the mind to drift into any picture or fantasy that is there. Then analyze it as you would a dream.

One woman saw a tray with five gold bars on it. Someone was handing her the tray. A week later she was notified that an uncle who owned a gold mine in Mexico had died and left her $50,000.

Warning: Do not do this metaphysical exercise more than the three cycles specified, nor more frequently than twice a week. It is recommended that when the exercise is performed on a regular basis, it be done only under the supervision of a qualified yoga teacher.

You Can Play a Part in World Politics Starting Today

Few of the leaders of the world today understand metaphysics. Abraham Lincoln, who was aware of the prophetic aspect of dreams and who felt the "presence" of his predecessors in the White House, probably gave more credence to these matters than twentieth century presidents.

When, in the late 1960's, Jose Silva, founder of Silva Mind Control, offered his program for developing psychic ability to the U.S.

government, it was politely refused with a "Don't call us, we'll call you" attitude.

Even the Soviets, who have been researching metaphysics in depth, probably have not begun applying metaphysical techniques on a political level to any great degree.

This places you in a unique position. If thousands were using these powers cn an international level, you could not be as effective. As it stands, you can use your metaphysical powers with often dramatic results. And if you can get others to join you in your efforts, you can increase your political leverage manyfold.

In India, lone mystics sit crosslegged on mountain heights in silence, days and nights on end. They are using their metaphysical power to bring peace and understanding to the world.

Western Alpha Picturing techniques are similar and often more effective.

Here are some of the pictures you can hold in mind while at the alpha level to assist world leaders in carrying out their responsibilities successfully:

- See the planet earth bathed in the light of love and material respect.
- See world leaders arriving in a huge stadium shaking hands, embracing and going about their work in the world arena in total harmony.
- See the White House. Send the President and his staff strength, wisdom, and understanding.
- See the leaders of two countries, who may be in a confrontation, meeting, shaking hands and arriving at mutual accord.
- See a particular political figure who appears to be mistaken or misled bathed in the light of enlightenment.

You can adapt these pictures to any political or social problem or crisis or you can create your own metaphysical picture to supply light, wisdom, goodness, righteousness, love, rapport, harmony, or whatever else is needed by the situation.

The action plan is as follows:

Metaphysical Action Plan To Help Solve Man's Problems on a Community or Planetary Level

1. Relax.
2. Alpha Picture the problem. See the picture dark. Hold it for only a few seconds.
3. Alpha Picture the solution. See harmony and accord. See this picture bathed in light. Dwell on it.
4. End relaxation knowing that progress has been made.

Important: Do not assume that any problem is too big for you. As a metaphysician, you are working on a level where numbers or geographical area are not the measure of size. If you see the problem as too big for you, that is the way it is. If you see yourself contributing to the solution, that is the way it is.

And your contribution may be more powerful than you think.

14

A System for Expanding Your Metaphysical Powers Day After Day for Greater Power, Infinite Riches, and Abounding Success

When you apply the methods unveiled in the previous chapters to your everyday life, you are wealthier than you were on the day you began reading Chapter 1. You are also:

- Able to control financial ups and downs.
- Able to attract members of the opposite sex at will.
- Able to exert effective leadership.
- Able to go wherever you want, whenever you want, instantly.
- Able to make good things happen day after day.

You are healthier, more energetic, more youthful. However, . . .Will you be able to expand or even repeat these benefits for yourself? Or will the magic fade away and leave you wondering how come you lost the "touch"?

How Karl J. Saw Proof of ESP But Denied It

A prominent game manufacturer, Karl J., said to me one evening, "I've got an open mind but I won't believe in ESP until I see it happen."

"Well, then, let's play a game that demonstrates ESP," I replied.

A volunteer was asked to leave the room while the rest of us decided on an object in the room and concentrated on it. We chose a lamp. Somebody was then asked to fetch the volunteer and to hold his hand as he entered the room. "I'll get him," offered Karl, and I could tell he figured he was preventing some skullduggery by taking care of that function himself.

The volunteer returned with Karl holding his hand, and after a moment of hesitation, walked directly to the lamp.

"Pretty good," said Karl. I let it go at that.

Several weeks later I was with Karl again when the subject of ESP came up. "Well," I said, "You saw proof."

"No," he replied, "I really led that person to the lamp myself."

When the mind does not accept what it sees, it grasps at any handy explanation.

This is a failing of United States scientists. Most turn up their nose at explaining metaphysical phenomena. Even in the Soviet Union, where the energies involved with consciousness and life forces are being thoroughly researched, a scientist recently exhorted his colleagues to spend more time studying UFO's and less time finding new ways to say they do not exist.

Know that you are a miracle worker. Don't let your friends "bug" you with "luck" or "coincidence" or "it was going to happen anyhow." Know that you are working with a very special energy which is just as dependable as electricity and which gets more and more powerful as you use it.

A person who denies the miraculous powers of metaphysics bars such powers from his life. The opposite is also true. *Key*: When you accept metaphysical "miracles" in your life, you demonstrate more and more metaphysical power.

Let cementing of your belief in your own metaphysical powers be *Step Number One* in your system for expanding these powers.

How to Use the Secret of the Five-Pointed Star to Magnify Your Metaphysical Powers

The star is on many flags. Most people consider that it is a symbol of higher aspirations. That might very well be so. But it goes further than that.

The five-pointed star is a symbol of man—the five points being his head, two arms, and two legs. When you stand in the posture of a star, you become a star among men.

Now I don't mean going around with your arms in the air and your legs apart. However, in the privacy of your room, once a day, preferably in the morning, become a "star" for a minute in the following manner:

Metaphysical Action Plan to Become a Star Among Men

1. Stand erect. Place your feet about two feet apart. Raise your arms to each side until they are half way between horizontal and pointing up.

2. Close your eyes. Picture a bright light, bigger and brighter than the sun, descending toward you from above.

3. Say aloud three times, "Universal life energy enters my body and surges through me as I go forth."

So powerful is this action that it is best not to perform it within hours of when you expect to retire. It accelerates your thinking, magnifies your awareness, intensifies your senses, assists physical functioning—and reinforces metaphysical powers.

One Place Where the Secret Star Action Works Every Day

Every weekday morning, a group of people perform this "star" action together on a beach in Waikiki. It is part of a program led by 94-year-old Paul Bragg, a dynamo of vigor and vitality, and chief founder of the natural health movement in the United States.

I was surprised to see this metaphysical exercise being done in a health group such as this. When I asked around about its effects, I got such comments as: "I get rid of those early morning doldrums in three seconds flat." "It's great for my back." "It helps me keep a positive attitude the rest of the day."

What most of his fans don't know is that Paul Bragg spent time in India studying at an ashram and has subtly imbued his program with metaphysical secrets such as this "star" action. One glance at these attractive youthful people of all ages convinces you that whatever they are doing, works.

A variation of this exercise can be used by you to concentrate restorative vitality to specific parts of your body:

Metaphysical
Action
Plan to
Concentrate
Universal
Life
Energy at
a Point in
Your Body

1. Hold your left arm as it is in the star posture, but turn the palm up more horizontally in a "receiving" position.

2. Place the right hand on whatever part of your body you wish to concentrate Universal Life energy. Placing your right hand on your forehead will enhance intellectual activities; on your solar plexus, general vital functioning; on the area of a specific organ, the vitality of its functioning, i.e.—stomach, lungs, or sexual areas.

3. Perform Steps 2 and 3 as described in the previous Action Plan.

Again it is not advisable to do the "star" action before retiring if you expect to fall asleep readily. It is an "awakening" exercise, one that will keep you energized for hours.

Most people who go to their alpha level while in a prone position fall asleep before they are able to perform their metaphysical work. However, doing the "star action" first enables you to lie down if you wish, while relaxing the body and slowing the mind, with a much lessened chance of dropping off.

Your *Step Number Two* in expanding your metaphysical powers is increasing the flow of Universal life energy through you. There are some other important factors that you can control for even greater metaphysical success.

How to Induce Signals
from Another Dimension

Metaphysicians have won some measure of respect from physicists in recent years largely because of biofeedback devices that measure physiological changes brought about by conscious effort.

The simple thermometer is, of course, the first biofeedback device. Then came the polygraph or lie detector equipment that measures the changes in skin galvanic action due to certain types of thoughts and emotions.

Today, brain waves are recorded on the encephalograph, which, coupled with a high gain amplifier, converts the impulses for audio monitoring. A person can now listen to his own brain waves slow down as he relaxes. This gives him confirmation that he is "doing it."

Metaphysical methods for relaxation and slowing of the brain are now confirmable by scientific observations. For those who need such confirmation, these devices are fine. But you have your built-in biofeedback mechanisms that you can use in many ways. Earlier in this book, we used the subconscious mind to send us back a number after our relaxation to indicate how deep we went. This is good to do from time to time to check on our relaxation effectiveness.

In the previous chapter, we learned how to invite a signal through our body to be used as a problem-solving code. Some feel this as a warmth, tingle, or shock. I use this "shock" or tingle method to reasure myself that I am in touch with "helping hands" on the other side of this manifest world. The Universal Consciousness works through its "parts" just as your own consciousness utilizes cells of your brain.

Since these entities or energies are involved in helping me—and you—it is comforting to know that when you are about to order something metaphysically, the help is there. It's something like saying: "Helpers, action alert!"

And the reply comes: "Roger. Standing by."

Don't cry "wolf." That is, don't test just to see if it works. Wait until you need to solve some problem, using your metaphysical powers.

Metaphysical Action Plan to Get a Signal That Help Is Standing by on Another Plane	1. Go to alpha. 2. Pause to request a signal as follows: "I am about to request assistance from higher energy. Please give me a signal, higher energy, if you are here and attuned to my consciousness. Give me a tingling sensation somewhere in my body." 3. Pause. You will then feel the sensation, if the energy is present.

Higher energies are usually there the moment your own consciousness pictures an outcome, result, or goal that you want to reach. Save the tingle test only for urgent matters where time is of the essence and a solution quite critical in nature.

Step Number Three in your system for expanding your metaphysical powers is developing these body reactions as a set of antennas to insure greater and greater success.

How to Rev Up Your Desire
for the High Voltage Power You Need to Attain It

You now know that the three most important factors that contribute to your power to perform metaphysical miracles in your life are:

- Desire. Feeling
- Deep level of mind.
- Detailed mental images.

These are the three D's that bring your dreamy wishes into 3-D, the three dimensional world. As you continue to use your metaphysical powers day after day they strengthen. However, you can accelerate the strengthening of those powers by:

- Increasing desire.
- Deepening your level of mind.
- Sharpening your mental picturing.

How John G. Heated Up His Desire
and Found Work Immediately

A young man named John G. came to me and said, "I don't have a job. I need to earn some money. What should I do?"

I detected that his tone was slightly skeptical. He might just as well have been saying, "OK, you're such a magician. Make a job appear for me."

"What have you done to find a job?" I asked him.

"Oh, I've asked around. But nobody knows of any openings."

John didn't want a job bad enough, I thought. "I don't want to promise you anything," I told him, "but check with me in a week." I figured he'd want a job even more by then.

In a week he returned, expecting I'd have an address or phone number for him. When I didn't, his jaw dropped.

"I'm down to my last dollar. I've really got to work."

That sounded more like it. Now I had something to work with. I taught him the simple Hermetic technique for heating desire up to the boiling point. In five minutes, he was so anxious to see it work, he dashed off without so much as a "See you."

John phoned me in three days. He had left me to walk around town. He hadn't gone three blocks when he passed a sign saying that a restaurant was opening soon. He walked around to the back. The owner was there. He hired him on the spot.

Hermes was an Egyptian metaphysician whose fame spread to Greece where his teachings were adopted by oracles and wise men. So secret were they that the word, *hermetic,* has come to mean "sealed" or "airtight."

Hermes is said to have originated this easy-to-use-method for heating up desire. You create a mental picture of your goal attained. If your goal is a job, as in the above incident, you must picture yourself working in such a job. My friend John did not necessarily want to work in a restaurant, so he pictured himself being handed a pay check. The picture you create should not be too restricting, but one that gives you the end product of what you want without spelling out the way it is to come about. Once you have decided on the picture, you proceed as follows:

Metaphysical Action Plan to Add Irresistible Voltage to Your Desire

1. Relax.

2. Breathe deeply, projecting that end goal image on to the air that you take into your lungs. It is as if your mind is a slide projector and you are projecting that goal image on the air as it enters your nostrils. You see the image riding on the air, entering your lungs and being carried to all the cells of your body.

3. (Optional.) To add even more voltage, project this image also on to the water you drink and the food you eat.

Do you want a different job? Then see yourself in that job. Project that image on to the air you breathe, the water you drink, the food you eat. See that image entering your very being. The job arrives.

Do you need a certain tool, fact, book, person? Then see yourself with that item or person. Project that image into air, water, food. Be ready for it to happen.

Do you have to make a train, bus or plane? See yourself making it. Project that image on the air you breathe as you rush. Watch it happen.

How Dr. Jacques B. Found a Rare Book He Needed by Using His Breath

A famous New York teacher of these powers, Dr. Jacques B., needed a rare out-of-print book. He was told he had to go to Canada to find it. Not wanting to spend the time and money in vain, he used this Hermetic image-projecting method. A few days after, as he was crossing Madison Avenue, he bumped into a man crossing in the opposite direction. The man dropped some books. As he helped him to pick them up, there was the rare book he was seeking.

Make the Hermetic image projection to rev up desire *Step Number Four* in your system for expanding your metaphysical powers as you move from success to even greater success.

The Intellect of a Genius is Only a Few Brain Waves Away for You

If you reexamine the ten levels of mind described earlier in this chapter, you see that as you approach a very deep level, such as that called #2, memory improves to the point that you can engage in something called age regression.

This is the ability to go back in time and remember things you could not possibly recall otherwise. You can remember the name of your teacher in the first grade, even if this means going back 50 years. You can even remember the names of the children who sat next to you in that class.

Well, you might say, of what use is that? None, probably. But this is only one change that takes place when you go to a deeper level of mind. All the bounds of logic seem to go down the drain, and the mind behaves in unbounded, unlimited ways.

In short, you become capable of performing mentally in a way that can be described as being "genius."

You might experience this in different ways. One woman is able to get flashes of exactly what the person she is talking to is about to say. Another woman that I know can see all the memory banks of a person and read that memory better than the person himself can remember.

A mathematician may see the answer to a complex problem flash on a screen before his eyes without having to go through lengthy computations. One can't help wonder if, perhaps, Tesla, electronic wizard of the early part of this century, used this method. He is purported to have been able to feed a complex mathematical problem into his mind and almost instantly "see" the answer.

Whatever the manner in which you experience wizard-like mental abilities, you can use them to your advantage in life ahead. The question is: How do you go to deeper and deeper levels of mind?

The more you practice metaphysics via Alpha Picturing, the

deeper you will go. But here is a technique to insure and accelerate that progress:

Metaphysical 1. Go to your alpha level and complete your metaphysi-
Action   cal work.
Plan to
Automatically 2. Give yourself the following programming: "Next
Deepen   time I go to these levels of mind, I will go deeper,
Alpha Levels   faster. Each experience at the alpha level will be bet-
                    ter and better."

3. End your session.

This is a built-in level deepener which, if you use it continually, is *Step Number Five* in your system for obtaining bigger and better metaphysical benefits as the days go by.

How to Add a New Dimension to Alpha Picturing to Escalate Its Power

The next step to complete the system for expanding your metaphysical powers focuses on your imaging.

So far, you have been imaging in a two-dimensional or "flat" way. Assuming your imaging is fairly good on this "screen" of your mind, you can move forward and expand your powers by the simple step of adding another dimension.

Three-dimensional Alpha Picturing is more effective than two dimensional Alpha Picturing. Then, when you master this and go into the next dimension, you are sending your consciousness into a world where time and space do not exist.

Some mystics have been able to do this. They can go anywhere instantly and, indeed, have been known to be in two places miles apart at the same time.

But that is getting beyond our scope. If we can master the three-dimensional picturing, we are attaining a miraculous power of consciousness, more than most people can comprehend. In fact, for those of you who feel you are not ready for the really "far-out," hold off reading the balance of this chapter until you have grown accustomed to your daily metaphysical miracles. Continue using two-dimensional or flat imaging of your mind, getting sharper and sharper pictures . . . until you are ready to take that one step beyond.

The rest of you, follow me.

The only way we can picture in three dimensions is to *be there*. Photographs, movies, TV—all substitutes for being there—are in two dimensions. To add that third dimension, you must consider that you are actually there. Instead of putting a person on a flat "screen" of your mind, you see that person as if you are in their room.

How I "Talked" to Helen and Helped Her Solve Her Marital Problem

Helen had left her husband Jack only a few months ago. He did not know where she was, and wanted her back. He asked me to send her positive messages of his love.

I went to my alpha level and asked to "see" Helen. There she was. I recognized the area. She was in an apartment of a girlfriend. I sent her the message from her husband. She turned her back on me. I decided to increase my effectiveness with a three-dimensional picture.

Instantly, I was "with her." I tapped her on the shoulder. She turned around. "What's wrong between you and Jack?" I asked.

"We don't communicate," she replied.

"Why?"

"He gives me orders. Never listens."

"That's the way men are, Helen. But suppose he listened, will you return?"

"Sounds impossible, but I will."

"Test him tomorrow after work. Phone him."

"I will."

I ended my alpha session and reported to Jack. He agreed to demonstrate his willingness to listen as well as talk, give and take. Sure enough, she called. Jack must have done his job well. They are still together at this writing.

You have to crawl before you can walk. It is easy to "be there" in your Alpha Picturing if you take it in easy steps. Here is a game to practice with:

1. Hold a piece of metal in your hand. Get the feel of it. Now put it down and mentally picture you are inside that metal. How does it feel? Check the smell. Are there any echoes? Knock on the wall; what does it sound or feel like?

2. Project yourself to a dog or cat you know—your pet or that of a friend or neighbor. Talk friendly to it. Pat it. Now check it out from the inside. Does it seem to have a healthy "feel"?

3. You are now ready to project yourself to some person you have a closeness to. Be there. See the details of the place. Pass right through the body if you wish, noting what you see; or, go right through the head, noting how you feel. You can be detecting the feelings of that person.

Step Number Six is three-dimensional picturing by "being there." The applications to improve your life are limitless. However, one warning. You cannot circumvent the Golden Rule. Do to others only as you would be willing that they do to you.

Key: Metaphysical powers used for evil boomerang on the perpetrator. Metaphysical powers used to solve human problems without doing any person harm bring multiplied benefits to the metaphysician.

How to Create
Magic Talismans with Strange Powers

We, as Americans, have suspected that staring can be felt. We stare at the back of the neck of a man in front of us in the elevator and he might turn around or else scratch his neck. Stare at a girl in a brief bathing suit as she walks by on the beach and watch her adjust her suit. U.S. Marines were trained during the Viet Nam war to detect someone staring at them in the jungle night.

This phenomenon can be understood better in the light of our precept, "Where consciousness goes, energy goes."

And it can be used to our advantage. Here's how.

For ages past, wise men and magic, or spiritual magicians, have created talismans—stones, gems, or objects that seem to have a very special power, such as bestowing health, luck, or riches.

From what you have already learned, you can create such a talisman. Remember the magic mirror you made? And the spell you placed in a stone? Put the book down and think about it for a minute. Can you figure out the method? Then read on and see how close you have come.

How to create a talisman:

Metaphysical Action Plan to Use the Power of Your Consciousness to Charge a Talisman

1. Select a semi-precious stone or mineral form that has been out in nature and not too close to any home or people.

2. Hold it in your hand. Go to your Alpha level of mind.

3. Project yourself (your consciousness) into the stone. Be there.

4. "See" Universal life energy pouring into the stone, lighting it up, filling it with the kind of power you want the stone to have (health-giving, love-radiating, wealth-attracting, etc.)

5. Seal this power in the stone by picturing yourself painting it with a "sealer." See the stone now as the source of Universal life energy.

Keep this stone with you when you work. Place it under your pillow at night. It will continue to work for you, emanating energy to you to augment your own energy, and helping to protect whomever you give it to.

Is creating a talisman your step number seven? No, but if you were willing to try to figure out the procedure before reading about it, you are applying step seven: Be creative. Apply what you now know to form your own methods for accomplishing metaphysical miracles in your life. Be metaphysically resourceful.

The resources of metaphysics are now yours. They are the greatest natural resources in the universe. With them you can literally create your own universe—a universe of love and plenty.

15

A Lifetime Plan for Using Miracle Metaphysical Power at the Right Time, in the Right Way, for Your Greatest Happiness

One day I was watching a team of four horses working on a timber farm in Maine. They would be hitched to a huge log—actually, a whole tree—which had been trimmed and floated down a stream. The team of horses would then pull the log up a short hill to where it was processed further.

One of the four horses seemed to have a mind of his own. He was always pulling to the side as if to change the team's direction. But of couse, he never did. All he really accomplished was to get himself twice as steaming hot as his teammates.

How like many of us. And a common trap for the metaphysician.

Swelled with the sense of power that comes with influencing other people, with changing events, and with causing improvements of physical conditions, the metaphysician can begin to pull against the team.

By that I mean, he can forget that he is hitched to a Cosmic or Universal Consciousness and is here not only to create his own universe, the microcosm, but to help create the larger Universe, the macrocosm.

Whenever your universe and the Universe do not "fit" or coincide, expect to sweat.

Twelve Cosmic Laws
That the Metaphysician Should Be Aware of

One of my first exposures to the world of metaphysics occurred some 25 years ago when I studied with Dr. Jacques Bustanoby, founder of Cosmo-Theosophy, a dynamic view of the universe. Dr. Bustanoby identified twelve major cosmic laws that you can see for yourself are in constant operation in both personal universes and the macrocosmic Universe.

This is the "flow." Know these laws and move with them in consciousness and your use of metaphysics becomes easier and easier, better and better, and increasingly rewarding.

Flout these natural laws and somehow the going becomes "uphill." You may succeed in your metaphysical action plans, but then reactions set in—and the perspiration begins. When your conscious activity is in line with Conscious Activity, you feel good. You have a peaceful feeling. You feel you are in control. You feel all is in order, not confused; balanced, not unbalanced; harmonious, not discordant. Your body, too, responds with feelings of health and wholesomeness.

Briefly, here are the twelve laws:

Law of Analogy. There is similarity without identity. The Bible says, "As above, as below." There is the microcosm and the macrocosm, the electrons rotating around the proton in an atom, the planets around the sun. There is man's consciousness and there is Universal Consciousness.

Law of Order. When a mind is orderly in its thinking, it is in accord with its Source, as the whole universe operates under orderly cause and effect. The more you are able to perceive the universe, the more you are able to see the orderly interrelationship of electrons, planets, and galaxies, and the orderly working together of plants, insects, animals, and man.

Law of Liberty. We enjoy as much liberty as we give. This is one of the most violated of laws—abused by husbands and wives, mothers and fathers, on up to labor, management, religion, and government. Attachment to things and people costs us our liberty. Only in complete self-reliance is complete freedom experienced.

Law of Concord. Humanity can be compared to a huge orchestra striving to produce some semblance of harmony. Concord is never at the sacrifice of expressing your unique self. But points of agreement should be seen and dwelt on rather than points of divergence. The universe is concordant, consistent, and congruous.

Law of Attraction. As vast as is the diversity of individual units, they all attract each other, proclaiming a oneness through an invisible handclasp. As human love emulates universal "love," it thrives.

Law of Balance. The perfect equipoise of the universe is the challenge for man—finding balance in satisfying the needs of the body, mind, and spirit, and in adjusting to the many polarities inherent in life.

Law of Creation. This is the calling into manifest form that which previously existed only in an invisible state. So, the metaphysician in all of us creates, much as the universe itself was created.

Law of Continuity. This is what is called evolution. First comes involution, then unfoldment. Each soul, or expression of life, manifest in a unique way, returns to the unseen, and manifests itself deathlessly.

Law of Compensation. This is the law behind cause and effect. Plant a carrot seed, and a carrot grows. We reap our just rewards. Secret motives are known by Universal Consciousness. There is no place to hide from this law, negatively or positively.

Law of Circulation. The universe is in constant motion. Wind currents, water cycles, and life incarnations are but a few of the circulatory movements, reflecting planetary, intragalactic, and galactic movements. Our personal life obeys this law—from blood to money.

Law of Vibration. Everything starts from Universal Consciousness and by the vibrations of energy becomes manifest. Matter is vibrating energy. Our senses of hearing, sight, taste, touch, and smell detect these vibrations. The metaphysician feels vibrations from people and from cosmic forces.

Law of Resiliency. The mighty oak is often less mighty than the resilient willow in a strong wind. "Agree quickly with thine adversary" is resiliency in action. Nature creates no irresistible forces or immovable bodies. The metaphysician bends to avoid breaks.

You Can Listen to the Universe and
Receive Intuitive Guidance to New Ideas and Inventions

Diogenes said, "We have two ears and one tongue in order that we may hear more and speak less."

Most of us are poor listeners to each other. If I were to tell you that the universe is talking to you, Mr. Metaphysician, right now, you would probably say, "Maybe, but I don't hear it."

Well, you heard me say it, and that could have been the voice of the universe. The universe speaks through people, events, signs, omens, and dreams. Some people even hear voices. But what does it all avail you, if you are a poor listener?

Most of us listen poorly because we are in the habit of being active. While we are supposed to be listening to another person, for instance, we are likely to be:

- Concerned with our own problems of the moment.
- Preparing a reply rather than attempting to understand.
- Daydreaming in between the words.
- Judging or reacting to prejudices and preconceptions.

We need to practice listening carefully to other people before we listen to the still voice of the universe.

How Nicholas Tesla Listened to the Universe's Secrets and Patented Them

At midnight, July 9, 1856, a boy was born to a Serbian Orthodox minister and his wife in Croatia, now part of Yugoslavia. Nikola Tesla, even in childhood, seemed to be in frequent meditation. When only five, he invented a water wheel, and a new kind of fish hook.

When Nikola was seven, firemen in the town were trying to pump water from the river for use on a fire, but no water came. Nikola, who was even then listening to the intelligence of the universe suddenly dived into the river and removed an obstruction that had crimped the hose.

Soon Tesla, in his twenties, invented and patented the first AC motor which he sold to George Westinghouse for a million dollars plus a partnership. Tesla went on to invent the wireless broadcast of radio waves, the turbine engine, and fluorescent lighting. He listened, invented, and patented.

But then the universe began to tell him secrets that man was not ready to accept, such as a way to charge up the earth so anyone could plug into it and get power. He was rejected by other scientists. He withdrew from society. So sensitive was he, that he could feel the rejections as negative energy. He could feel other people's pain and emotions. He lived his last years as a recluse insulating his hypersensitive attunement from both men and the universe.

There is a listening trigger device used in many Eastern cultures. It consists merely of placing the thumb and forefinger together, forming a circle. This has a dual purpose:

1. It closes your energy circuit so you no longer transmit, but are free to receive.

2. It symbolically unites your will with the Universal Will, thus tuning you to this highest "station" and inviting intuitive reception.

Here is how to institute or "set" this triggering device:

Metaphysical Action Plan to Sensitize Intuitive Reception

1. Relax deeply.

2. Hold thumb and forefinger of left hand (if you are left-handed, the right hand,) together to form a circle, with the other fingers extended.

3. State mentally, "Every time I hold these two fingers together, I am able to concentrate easily and automatically on what a person is saying, and I can understand, and remember. I am also able to listen to the intuitive messages of the universe and receive them loud and clear."

4. Repeat daily for several days.

5. When listening to another person, place the two fingers together.

6. When in quiet, relaxed moments, place the two fingers together, and be aware of all ideas that drift into your mind.

The Colors That People
Radiate And What They Mean

You are about to make a sale—you hope. You are waiting for the right moment to clinch it.

You are about to make a "pass" at a member of the opposite sex.

You are waiting for the moment when you might have the best chance to succeed.

You are about to make a suggestion to your neighbor that eliminates a nuisance to you. You are waiting for the right moment when he will take it graciously and cooperatively.

How would you like to be able to see a "traffic light" under such circumstances, which stayed red until the right moment arrived, and then it turned green? Well, there is a system of color signals that radiate from the human body. It is called the aura.

This human aura has been seen by metaphysicians for millennia. However, in recent years, it has been photographed. Scientists can now observe changing colors in the human aura. It all started with Semyon Kirlian, a Russian electrician, who quite accidently discovered that photographing the human hand with high voltage electricity instead of light yielded a luminescent "shadow" that followed the contours of the fingers. He developed this principle in many ways, took out 14 patents, and soon was able to photograph the energy field around a person in color.

It proved to be a fantasia of multicolored lights, brilliant flares, subtle clouds, and wandering pinpoints. It has opened up a whole new horizon of knowledge on the energy body of the human being and promises to dovetail with the recent upsurge of interest in acupuncture and its energy medians.

You do not have to be a Kirlian to photograph these energy fields. Simple crystal sets[1] are on the market that create the necessary 15,000 to 20,000 volts by merely pressing a spring release. Since only a tiny current flows, they are perfectly safe.

You do not even have to be a metaphysician to see auras. But now that you are one it is doubly easy. In a moment, I will show you how. You will not be able to see all the subtle nuances but you will be able to see the dominant color. And it is this dominant color that can be your "red" or "green" light.

Here are the main colors and what they usually connote:

- *Red*. High emotion. Could be an angry person or one with the passion of erotic love.
- *Orange*. Socially inclined. Seeks the security of group activity. Likes to work with others.

[1]Systecon, P.O. Box 417, West Hyattsville, Maryland, 20782.

- *Yellow*. An intellectual person. Emphasis is on continuing mental action rather than on decisive physical action.
- *Green*. Tranquility, with power. This is the color of materialism— both acquisition of wealth and attention to health.
- *Blue*. A spiritual color, usually indicating a thoughtful, considerate person.
- *Violet*. This end of the color spectrum leads to inner mysteries. This is the philosophical person, the poet, the visionary.

How to Begin to See Auras and Profit by Them

If you would like to see auras, I have news for you: You have been seeing them all your life. Your eyes have been seeing them but your brain has been rejecting the information. All you have to do now is to retrain your mind to accept what is there.

Begin by looking at the hair outline of a person. The head is where the aura can be most easily seen and close to the head is where it is at its greatest strength or visibility.

You will notice that there is "condition" at this point. It is like a poor print job where the color register is not perfect. Your eye adjusts for the poor color printing where one color overlaps another and you don't notice it unless you look for it. Similarly, your eye has been adjusting for the aura color at the hair line.

Concentrate at this point just above the hair line. Analyze what it is that appears to blur the "picture" at this point. Look past the head at the wall or curtain background. You will begin to see a color "cast" that both interferes with the hair line and the backdrop. It is as if you were seeing through a colored piece of plastic. The color is the radiating aura.

Since this is a retraining to accept rather than to reject, you must accept whatever you see. If you think you see something, accept what you think you see.

The person who tries to see auras in this manner and reacts with "I can't" might just as well give up. He is only reinforcing what his mind has already accomplished for him years ago. On the other hand, the person who grabs hold of any little visual aberration and makes an effort to expand on it is retraining himself to accept the sight of auras.

How Sterling B. Saw an Aura
That Saved the Day for Him

Sterling B. was a public relations man who because of his interest in metaphysics trained himself to see auras as well as to pick up information from objects (psychometry). An opportunity arose for him to win an important client, an active member in the Chamber of Commerce. Representing such a client would certainly bring him more business from its membership, so Sterling was particularly anxious to come up with a convincing presentation. He went overboard in preparing a proposal that included some original promotional ideas he was quite proud of. He was going to bet all his "chips" on the first meeting with the Chamber's directors.

The meeting started with the usual statement of aims by the directors and the usual recital of qualifications by Sterling. The moment had come for Sterling to play his ace in the hole, but he kept receiving strange feelings about one of the directors. He looked at his aura and saw that it was red.

He decided to hold off. He said he was not ready, but offered to make his presentation to individual directors prior to their next meeting. They agreed. Sterling found out meanwhile that the director with the red aura had been acting as the promoter ever since the resignation of the last public relations man, and in fact had caused that resignation. He resented an outside man being brought in when he could be doing the job.

Sterling made the rounds individually, but avoided the director. At the next meeting, Sterling apologized that time did not permit seeing this one director. The vote for Sterling was unanimous, with one director abstaining.

As you begin to see auras—as slight tinges of color at first, then as more discernible hues—you gain insight into other people and are able to control your timing on matters for a greater chance of success.

Here are optimum colors for special actions:

- To make a sale—orange or green.
- To get a favorable business decision—blue or green.
- To win a member of the opposite sex—blue or red, providing there is no anger or fear (a combination of these colors, rose, is excellent).
- To ask a favor—blue or orange.
- To ask advice—yellow.

People's auras change. I have often asked a person with a strong green or blue aura to step to the front of the class so the students can view it, only to find the aura pale yellow as the person became self-conscious.

These changes can take place from minute to minute, or day to day.

The more you look at auras, and the more you accept what you see, the more you will see. However, you can accelerate this process with this metaphysical reinforcement:

Metaphysical Action Plan to Bring Auras More Clearly Into View	1. Look at a person's aura. Remember what little you see, even if it is only a fuzziness.
	2. As soon as possible, retire to privacy, relax, and visualize that person, recalling what you saw of the aura.
	3. Reach forward with your right hand to an imaginary rheostat. Turn it clockwise, knowing it will brighten the aura picture, color and all.
	4. Accept whatever improvement takes place.
	5. Mentally repeat, "I restore my ability to see auras. It returns brighter and in color, better and better every day."
	6. End action plan.

How to Use a Television Screen to See the Future

The human mind operates in a spaceless and timeless dimension as well as here and now. That is why you can Alpha Picture and see what is happening miles away even if it already happened or is about to happen. And that is why dreams are frequently glimpses of the future.

Stephen B. Saw the Outcome of the Trial a Year Ahead

Stephen B. was a practitioner of Alpha Picturing, getting better and better every day, when one of his real estate deals hit a snag. The seller reneged on the deal months later due to a tenant problem and a rise in values, sending back the deposit money. Stephen B. took the seller to court but as in most areas, the court calendar was jammed and the case would not come up for a year.

Stephen B. needed to plan his cash flow so that he would be

prepared either way. He used his Alpha Picturing to look ahead to the final day of the court proceedings. He heard the judge rule in his favor, solving the tenant problem in a special way. Stephen B. planned ahead as if this were indeed true. When the trial came up and all testimony was in, the judge made exactly the ruling Stephen had foreseen, including the handling of the tenant in that very special way.

In a previous chapter you imbued a mirror with special metaphysical properties that enabled you to see miles away. You can now use that mirror to see into the future, too. However, I personally prefer to use a television set and a clock. I'll tell you why.

Metaphysical abilities exist in all people. Metaphysical teachers and metaphysical books merely serve to "open" or activate these otherwise dormant abilities. This education is in its purest form, as the word education derives from the Latin, "to lead out."

These metaphysical abilities are brought out more easily by our doing things we are accustomed to doing. Actually, the mirror could be a crystal ball, but we are not used to looking into a crystal ball. Any piece of shiny surfaced material would do.

One drawback about such a device is that we are accustomed to merely a reflection. What carries us a step forward is a television screen. We are accustomed to looking into it and seeing something other than what is in the room being reflected. So the television screen is a useful metaphysical lever. So is a clock. Or a calendar. We are going to use all three, in a special way, to "see" the future.

Metaphysical
Action
Plan to Use
a Television
Set, Clock,
or Calendar
to See the
Future

1. Place a clock on your television set and prop up a calendar, both facing you as you sit in front of the television screen.

2. Close your eyes, relax, and deepen your relaxation.

3. Mentally see the calendar at the month and year you wish to perceive. Mentally turn the clock to the time of the day you are interested in.

4. Mentally see the television screen (still with your eyes closed) and mentally turn on the set as you ask mentally, "I wish to see the_____(state situation in the future)."

5. Wait patiently as mental pictures drift across the television screen. Accept and remember what you see.

6. Turn set off mentally, and mentally reset calendar to today, and clock to now, as you end your action.

How to Move Ahead in Life to
Surpass Even the Person You Most Admire

Through metaphysics you can set goals and reach them. There are also other ways to do this. You can do the same by the sweat of your brow. There is nothing wrong with this way. It is the traditional concept of true progress. But the metaphysical way is easier.

No sweat.

When you do your job the best way you know how, hoping to get ahead, that's fine. You will. But you are working on physical energy. It tires you. When you do your job the best way you know how while at the same time Alpha Picturing to get ahead, you have life energy working for you. You never get to know what the word *tired* means.

Life energy seems to get the work done *for* you in addition to *by* you. Everything seems to go right. Somehow other people inadvertently help you. It is as if you are a part of a team instead of working alone.

Back in the 1960's, the Russians loaded a brood of baby rabbits on a submarine, keeping the mother ashore hooked up to an encephalograph. With the submarine deeply submerged, and out of all possible radio contact, the baby rabbits were killed one by one. Each time one was killed, the mother rabbit's brain recorded it.

This kind of survival communication has been measured in many species of plant and animal life. What has not yet been measured is the flow of less urgent communication that appears to be going on.

This communication could be on a lower level than Universal Mind or Cosmic Mind. It could be on a level of what psychologists in the past have called a *group mind* or *mass consciousness*.

When an ant radial highway to an important food source is blocked, the signal instantly reaches a "police battalion" that could be hundreds of yards away but which then heads out to clear the obstruction. It seems doubtful that this intelligence had to pass through the Universal Mind. It seems more logical that it was an "inside job," internal to the Ant Consciousness—that is, on the ant wave length.

So it is with human problems. Where human goals are involved, picturing them activates the Universal Mind where outside factors are involved—weather, crops, circumstances—but where other people are involved, or even just yourself, it is Human Consciousness that is activated.

Life energy on the humankind wavelength is then turned on, and its flow sweeps you to your goal. Here is a special way to use it that can vault you into realms of success so rapidly it can take your breath away.

Is there somebody in your creative line of work that you admire and would like to equal, even surpass? This could be:

- Rembrandt in art.
- Beethoven in music.
- Jesus in spiritual growth.
- Gibran in writing.
- Rockefeller in finance.
- Henry Ford in manufacturing.
- Shakespeare in drama.
- Jung in psychiatry.
- Nightingale in nursing.

If you select a "pedestal" figure in your line, be it selling, marketing, or production, you can activate Human Consciousness to make you equal to that person, *plus*. Here is how:

Metaphysical Action Plan to Surpass the Greatest Person that You Know of in Your Field

1. Relax very deeply.
2. See the person you wish to emulate and surpass. You need not visualize the features. See that person at work in a typical setting. See his or her successful results.
3. Repeat mentally, "Human Consciousness is moving me. I become as (insert name). And I surpass (insert name) in accomplishment by adding my own uniqueness." Say a total of three times.
4. See yourself in a typical setting. See your successful results.
5. End your relaxation, knowing you are now "programmed" for a brilliant success.

I have seen artists change overnight, producing in their own style, but at a high talent level, when they did this metaphysical work. A teacher I know who chose Jesus to emulate and surpass has become a respected guru-type in less than a year.

What to Do in Case
of Emergency for Miraculous Survival

Did you ever try to kill a carpenter ant only to watch the smashed bit gradually unfold, move its legs, and then walk away, perhaps dragging one leg, but even this soon, normalizing? Ant Consciousness seems to flow into a mangled ant and miraculously heal it. Human Consciousness, working with Universal Consciousness, can be triggered by tragedy or calamity into miraculous action, too.

How Mrs. Michele B. Survived What
Could Have Been a Fatal Crash

Mrs. Michele B. was driving her economy car along a mountain road when a speeding truck crossed an intersection and hit her broadside. In the instant that she šaw the truck out of the side of her eye, Michele turned her thoughts to the Higher Consciousness. This activated the Human and Universal Consciousness. For some reason the impact was not as thunderous as she expected. Her car did not overturn. She sat as if in a trance. She felt at peace. Other cars stopped. She was taken to a hospital. The leg she had on the brake pedal suffered a severe fracture. But there were few marks from the accident and the leg soon healed.

How Harry Houdini Called on
Superhuman Forces to Save Him

When the famous magician Harry Houdini was dropped through a hole in the ice in the Hudson River, handcuffed and hog-tied, the crowd watched horrified for many minutes beyond survival time with no appearance by the magician.

What Houdini had not counted on was his inability to cope with the river's current. By the time he had freed himself he was hundreds of yards downstream from the hole which would permit him to surface.

Had Houdini used his personal strength to swim back upstream through the ice cold waters, this tale would have had a different ending. But he turned it over to Higher Consciousness. Instead of swimming, he was "swam" and in a few minutes appeared before a relieved crowd of admirers.

People succumb to accidents unnecessarily. They tense up in the fear of the moment. Metaphysicians often survive accidents that would be the demise of others. This is not because they have a magic ointment or invoke other magic powers. Metaphysicians survive what could otherwise be fatal accidents because they turn the job over to higher authority.

Metaphysical Action Plan to Survive a Cataclysm or Accident

1. Do this action plan now to prepare for any eventuality. Relax.
2. Turn eyes upward. Mentally state, "When I turn my eyes upward, I surrender my Higher Self to the Will of Human Consciousness and Universal Consciousness."
3. End session. Repeat daily for a week.
4. Should you be involved in a cataclysm or accident, keep eyes open and working until the moment is no longer optically critical, then turn eyes upward and relax.

Know this: Turning your eyes upward has always stimulated your brain's alpha output. It does so for everyone. What you have reinforced metaphysically is your "partnership" with a higher consciousness.

The True Meaning
of Your Metaphysical Power

You can now do many things which you once thought—and many still think—impossible.
You can:

- Change your luck.
- Turn enemies into friends.
- See through walls.
- Control the opposite sex.
- Manifest prosperity.
- Dissolve physical problems.
- Extend youth.
- Relieve pain without drugs.

- Control the weather.
- Create powerful talismans.
- Send thoughts thousands of miles.
- Detect thoughts and feelings.
- Create a magic mirror.
- Exert influence over others.
- Protect yourself from psychic attack.
- Locate hidden treasure.
- Mine for gold and minerals.
- Get answers from the cosmos.
- Induce meaningful visions.
- Survive an emergency.
- See forward and backward in time.

The key chapters in turning on your metaphysical powers have been Chapters 1, 2, and 3. The key chapter in strengthening them as you use them has been Chapter 4.

The key to your success in life as a metaphysician is your motive. Seek to solve your problems without causing problems to others. Seek to use metaphysical powers to help others, too.

I have a stake in your success. If I have revealed powers that you will use to make this a better world to live in, I gain "points" with the Universe. If these powers are abused by you, I stand to lose points. Naturally, I have used my own metaphysical powers to encourage proper use, and discourage improper use. Indeed, should you try to use these powers for evil, they will not work.

These powers are awesome indeed. With them you can help man's happiness, health, and prosperity anywhere on this planet. And the more you help others, the more you will find the powers work for your good, too. These are the "points" that you earn and that bring you miraculous dividends.

If you glance at the aforementioned list again, you will note certain characteristics about your consciousness,

1. When you transcend air distances with your consciousness, you are being *infinite*.

2. When you transcend any time, past or present, with your consciousness, you are being *eternal*.

3. When you can "pick up" any information you need, you are being *omniscient*.

4. When you can correct problems and control circumstances, you are being *omnipotent*.

Infinite. Eternal. Omniscient. Omnipotent.
Does this give you insight into who you really are?
Farewell, Metaphysician.